How the Peace was Won

How the Peace was Won

Brian Rowan

Gill & Macmillan

Gill & Macmillan Ltd
Hume Avenue, Park West, Dublin 12
with associated companies throughout the world
www.gillmacmillan.ie

978 07171 4486 0

Type design: Make Communication
Print origination by Carole Lynch
Printed and bound by in Great Britain by MPG Books Ltd, Bodmin, Cornwall

This book is typeset in Linotype Minion and Neue Helvetica.

The paper used in this book comes from the wood pulp of
managed forests. For every tree felled, at least one tree is
planted, thereby renewing natural resources.

A CIP catalogue record for this book is available
from the British Library.

5 4 3 2 1

Contents

Acknowledgments

Politics and politicians change, and this book takes us inside the most remarkable chapter yet in Northern Ireland's peace process. It is the story of how Ian Paisley and Martin McGuinness came to do business, a story told through many different voices and from many different angles. I have been fortunate in my reporting of the political and security situation in the North to be able to speak to all sides. Many of them have made their thinking and their words available to me for the pages of *How the Peace was Won*, for this book on how a process of conflict resolution brought enemies together in new beginnings and new relationships.

I want to thank Martin McGuinness, Gerry Kelly, Ian Paisley Junior, Sir Hugh Orde, Gusty Spence, Peter Sheridan, Harold Good, John de Chastelain, Tauno Nieminen, Andrew Sens, Aaro Suonio, Lord Alderdice, Alex Attwood, Danny Morrison, Peter Hain, Brendan Duddy and the many others for the contributions they have made. There are, of course, people I cannot name—loyalist, republican, security force and political sources whose information I have relied on for many years, but who wish their contributions to remain anonymous. I also want to thank Kate Turner and Brandon Hamber from the Healing Through Remembering project for sharing their thinking with me as I have reported the next steps after the war. Their thoughtful research examines and offers suggestions on how we can make peace with the past.

This book is dedicated to the memory of David Ervine, a close friend who died suddenly in January 2007. In a place long known for its divided communities and its two sides, we kicked with different feet. That is the peculiar Northern Ireland way of saying that we were of different religions. Ervine was part of the war and an even bigger part of the peace, but what made him different was his openness and honesty about his past. He admitted his role in the Ulster Volunteer Force, not in any boastful way but more as a statement of fact. He knew that war had delivered no winners and that the future had to be hewn out of politics and peace. His funeral—a celebration of his life—and those who attended it said a lot about his contribution to what we now have in Northern Irish society.

In this book I describe the thin line I have been asked to walk during my reporting career, a career in which I have depended on the advice of some outstanding journalists and great friends, including David McKittrick, Eamonn Mallie, Deric Henderson, Seamus Kelters, Mervyn Jess and Andrew Colman. They often accuse me of not listening, but they are always there when I need them and for that I will always be grateful. After many years at the BBC I now work as a freelance writer and broadcaster, and I make regular contributions to the war and peace debate on the pages of the *Belfast Telegraph*. I want to thank its editor, Martin Lindsay and also Paul Connolly and Ronan Henry for always making space available to allow me to say my bit.

This book emerged out of an approach by Marshall Matchett and then a meeting with Fergal Tobin of Gill & Macmillan. The editor, Rachel Pierce, made a valuable contribution and the gentle nudges of Deirdre Rennison Kunz have kept me on my toes in the period leading to publication. I want to thank all at Gill & Macmillan for their professionalism and commitment to this project. I also want to thank my cousin, the photographer Marie Therese Hurson. Jim McDowell introduced me to journalism in 1981 and sent me on my way with encouraging words. He has also spoken angry words to me when he has felt they were needed. His friendship is something I will always value, and I will never forget the break he gave me all those years ago. Back then, I never imagined that I would end up reporting some of the most significant developments in recent history—the ceasefires, decommissioning, the end of the IRA's war and the republican endorsement of policing. It has been a privilege to be a part of that. It has also been a huge challenge.

My family have given me all the space and all the support I needed to do my work and they have lived with the risk that is involved when you report a conflict while living in the middle of it. Val, Ruairi, Elle and PJ have kept me sane, kept me going and gave me so much encouragement and help when I took a nervous first step into the world of election politics in 2007.

Northern Ireland's war is over: that is the message that is sounded loudest in this book. Political leaderships will change and have changed. In the months leading to the publication of *How the Peace was Won*, Tony Blair, Bertie Ahern and Ian Paisley handed things over to Gordon Brown, Brian Cowen and Peter Robinson. But the peace has been made—and made possible— because in the end people were prepared to talk. Words not bullets are what worked; dialogue triumphed over the gun. That is the message and the lesson that should be taken from our peace process and from this book.

Brian Rowan
June 2008

Prologue
The cat and the car

There were many mornings when I told the kids that I was looking for the cat under Mummy's car. It was my way of not frightening them; it was the war and my work playing inside my head—making me think about and look for the bomb. I don't know if I ever expected to actually find something, but if anything had happened and I hadn't looked, I would never have forgiven myself. This was something that people never saw. It was part of living in a conflict and reporting it, and then having to go home, and, at home, doing what I could to keep my family safe.

My daily work was the business of codewords, of statements from the IRA and the loyalist organisations, of talking to the security forces, trying to interpret, trying to understand, trying to explain. It was a precarious walk along the thinnest of lines and, at times, it was both a physical and a mental struggle. There were moments when I wanted to walk away—sometimes run away—moments when I questioned the morality of what I was doing, and was unsure of the answer. Often the statements I was given were about killing and the codeword was the sign that authenticated the communication—Titanic, Cromwell, Crucible, Braveheart, Defender, Boomerang, Arafat, Pale Horse, Genesis and Paschendale. These were the hidden words of the war. Now, they act as an *aide memoire*—how I remember some of the killings. I knew the codewords, and many times I knew the caller. These statements were a précis of life and death— cold words that gave the explanation behind the killing, the reason and, many times, they were the means of making the next threat, before the next bomb exploded or bullet was fired.

I want to set out two such statements from 1992, copied from my original notes and issued in the name of the UDA-linked Ulster Freedom Fighters (UFF), an organisation that formally ended its war some fifteen years later, on Remembrance Sunday 2007. I am not sure if the full text of either of these statements has ever before been published:

April 1992: The UFF acting on top grade intelligence carried out this morning's assassination of female PIRA member Philomena Hanna, sister of Sinn Féin/PIRA member Richard McAuley. The UFF and the loyalist people have seen as recently as last week the central role females are playing within the republican war machine. The UFF wish to state once again that we make no distinction between male and female members of PIRA. The government and the Northern Ireland Office should take note that no amount of failed security force policies will deter us from ridding Ulster of the cancer of republicanism once and for all.

November 1992: The UFF admit responsibility for today's attack on the bookmaker's shop at Oldpark Road. Direct responsibility for the UFF carrying out such attacks lies with Sinn Féin and the Provisional IRA. The UFF warned last week what we would do if PIRA continued their sectarian attacks. Today we acted accordingly. We again warn Sinn Féin and PIRA that the theatre of war will be full of casualties from the republican community in the coming weeks.

Those are just two documents in a mound of such communications and contacts, and just two stories that tell how twisted and random this war could be. Philomena Hanna was not Richard McAuley's sister and was not a member of the Provisional IRA

(PIRA), but that was the label used in the attempt to justify this particular killing. In a radio news report at the time, I said the following:

> The family of the Catholic mother of two murdered by the UFF yesterday have rejected the terrorists' claim that she was in the IRA. Philomena Hanna was shot dead in the Springfield Road chemist shop where she worked. Attempting to justify this killing the UFF claimed the attack was carried out as a result of what it called 'high-grade intelligence'. The terrorist group alleged its victim was a member of the IRA and said it believed Philomena Hanna was a sister of Sinn Féin's Richard McAuley. But in many quarters these claims have been rejected as absolute nonsense. Richard McAuley said the murdered woman wasn't a relative and accused the UFF of attempting to excuse what he called 'the cold-blooded sectarian murder of an innocent mother'. Sinn Féin also said there were telephone calls to two of its offices after the shooting. The callers said they were journalists and asked for the name of the murder victim. Sinn Féin suspect these calls were made by loyalists attempting to identify who'd been killed. The official RUC line described the shooting as 'blatantly sectarian', and one senior police officer I spoke to called it 'unbelievably callous'.

You can read in the words of that broadcast that these statements were never simply reported. As best we could, my colleagues and I tested the information and the claims made, for example the label attached to the victim, which on many occasions was a character assassination. I think more about these things now than I did then, probably because I have more time to think and reflect than I did in those days of killing when people became statistics and one death merged into the next. The fog that shrouded the war is lifting now and I can see and hear more clearly.

I took scores of those statements about the fight, and then about the peace. They are scraps of paper and scribbled notes, part of the logbook of that very long war. They are as cold as the killings—words that add to the hurt of so many families. These were despatches from behind the lines: the claim and counter-claim, the fact and the fiction.

I have known Richard McAuley for most of my working life. He was a member of the IRA, but today is identified as Gerry Adams' closest aide, a member of the republican 'kitchen Cabinet' that thought its way out of war and into peace. I spoke to him for this book and we talked about that statement in 1992, about the death of Philomena Hanna and about his thoughts, then and now:

> I was thinking to myself, if I go to this family, what do you say to them, and I remember thinking at the time, how would you even broach any of that? When I heard that statement and the excuse that was made, my first thought was for the woman and her family. It was a particularly vicious action against a mother, and the excuse was so transparently pathetic. And my other thought was for my own family, because while this was quite clearly a flimsy excuse, I do have sisters and here they were hearing something about somebody being killed supposedly because she was my sister. It was one of those moments when an action goes beyond the news and the headlines.

I think I understand what he means. There were hundreds and thousands of these statements over the three decades of what came to be called the Troubles, but what made this one different for Richard McAuley was that *his* name was included, that he was used as part of the excuse for this killing on this day.

The attack on the bookmaker's shop, described in the second statement given above, was every bit as indiscriminate as the

Hanna shooting: a door opened, gunfire, a grenade explosion and three men lay dead, one of them an elderly man of seventy-two years, a veteran of the Second World War. It was random, unthinking, devastating. After the gunfire and the explosion came the statement, which was a routine part of the regular contact I had with this organisation, among others. On this occasion the codeword used was 'Crucible'. It had been in use for a while. A senior loyalist told me they had looked it up in the dictionary because they had wanted to use a word that meant something in the context of their war.

When you read your own name in one of those coded statements from one of those organisations, it made you think and worry even more. The solicitor Rosemary Nelson was killed in a booby-trap bomb explosion in March 1999. The device had been concealed beneath her car. At the time, the killing was claimed in the name of the Red Hand Defenders, but it was members of the Loyalist Volunteer Force (LVF) who had placed the bomb. I reported that fact, and the LVF issued a response:

May 1999: We maintain the view that only a political imbecile or one intent on causing new levels of mayhem in the country would put forth the statement that Brian Rowan and the BBC have made yesterday. We therefore call upon both parties to retract the statement or name the source of their so-called intelligence.

Over the years I read many, many people's names in coded messages, but this one, containing my own name, had a very different impact. It made me think more about what could happen—think more about the risks and the potential threat. When you live in a conflict and report it, you are asked to make very difficult judgments and decisions: what to do, what not to do, what to say, what not to say, what is right, what is wrong. As I said, it is the thinnest line.

So, how do journalists negotiate that line? The answer is you learn from experience, and you make mistakes. You have to walk that line to know what to do and some of what you hear along the way leaves you frightened of talking in your sleep. I thought that if I left my position with the BBC, I could walk away from all of it. But I have found it is not that simple. It was my decision to leave the BBC in December 2005 and a reporting role that left me, too many times, between a rock and a hard place. What do you say to the police officers investigating a murder when they come looking for access to your telephone records? I had to say no, and in this book I will explain why. At times that thinnest of lines just vanished, and it left me lost. There were dilemmas and impossible decisions that people never knew about, times when, for all the support I knew I had, I still felt I was on my own, with only my gut instinct to guide me.

This book is not a chronological walk through the last forty years in Northern Ireland's history. It is a personal reflection that will explore those moments that changed our political and security landscape forever. What transformed our war into peace? Who made it possible? And what are we to do by way of remembering all that must never be forgotten? These are the questions I want to examine and, hopefully, answer.

Ian Paisley and Martin McGuinness travelled a vast distance to their meeting place in Northern Ireland's government, and the truth is that it has been a remarkable journey that offers a template of hope to conflict zones across the world. Northern Ireland's recent history has proved that even the most intractable wars can be brought to an end and that enemies can become, not friends, but partners in the processes of politics and peace. This doesn't quieten the cries of the dead, however, nor of the living. Peace does not give back the lives that were taken. The many sides I spoke to took many lives and on occasion they told me why. Those statements, so often offered glibly as an excuse for murder, need to be revisited now. Our truth process, if there ever is such, could prove to be as ugly as the war that gave rise to it, which is perhaps why there are those who don't want to engage on this level. Here, I will argue for a table of explanation that will allow the peace to ask its questions of the war. It can work only if all sides are present, not just the IRA and the loyalists. There are questions for politicians, for governments, for the Churches and the media and for the security forces, and there is the horrible underlying truth of collusion and of the war games that cost lives. It is all part of the record of this war. How much of it will be explained, and who will come to that table of explanation?

The war is over. The question now is: how do we make peace with the past?

Chapter 1

Stormontgate

The background to this case [Stormontgate] is that a paramilitary organisation, namely the Provisional IRA, *was actively involved in the systematic gathering of information and targeting of individuals. Police investigated that activity and a police operation led to the recovery of thousands of sensitive documents which had been removed from government offices. A large number of people were subsequently warned about threats to them.*
(STATEMENT FROM POLICE SERVICE NORTHERN IRELAND (PSNI), 8 DECEMBER 2005, THE DAY THE 'STORMONTGATE' CASE COLLAPSED IN COURT.)

My name is Denis Donaldson. I worked as the Sinn Féin Assembly group administrator in Parliament Buildings at the time of the PSNI *raid on the Sinn Féin offices in October 2002—the so-called Stormontgate affair. I was a British agent at the time. I was recruited in the 1980s after compromising myself during a vulnerable time in my life … I was not involved in any republican spyring at Stormont. The so-called Stormontgate affair was a scam and a fiction.*
(STATEMENT MADE 16 DECEMBER 2005, EIGHT DAYS AFTER THE 'STORMONTGATE' CASE COLLAPSED IN COURT.)

*If only we were that good. The notion that we are
that sophisticated and that organised and could plan
that sort of event in that sort of way is such crazy
stuff. It is laughable.*
(PSNI CHIEF CONSTABLE SIR HUGH ORDE SPEAKING
IN SEPTEMBER 2007 TO DISMISS CLAIMS THAT
'STORMONTGATE' WAS CONCOCTED BY THE
'SECUROCRATS'.)

This opening chapter is the story of an intelligence-gathering scandal linked to the IRA, which came to be known as 'Stormontgate'. Its importance is that it brought down a government—the power-sharing Executive built on fragile foundations after the Good Friday Agreement of 1998. The continuing risk to life prevents me from writing all I know about this episode, but I want to set out here the cat-and-mouse play of the intelligence world. It is the behind-the-scenes story of Stormontgate, as much as it can be told at the present time.

The home of a man whom I will call Mr X is at the centre of a surveillance and bugging operation. It is what the IRA would consider a 'safe house' or safe hiding place. The Stormontgate papers—political documents and correspondence—are hidden there, but the story is out; the Special Branch knows. How did they find out? A friend of Mr X had become a police informer. In 2002 the Special Branch considered moving this man out of Northern Ireland, and they may consider doing so again. When they took him across their lines and into the dirty war, he became their responsibility and his life was immediately at risk. To be found out playing this game is to be the next 'collaborator'. This man is the informer on the scandal that broke a government. This man was not Denis Donaldson, who is now dead.

It is a costly lesson to learn that there are some things that are never forgiven. Even when war becomes peace, 'traitors' still wind up dead. The breaking news on the evening of 4 April 2006 concerned Denis Donaldson, a Belfast republican, who had been shot dead at a cottage in a remote area in County Donegal. During the war, one group or another would have admitted responsibility quickly and outlined why they had done it. Not so in peacetime. The people who know who was responsible for the death of Denis Donaldson are not saying.

I knew Denis Donaldson for many years and yet, like so many others, I did not know him at all. Donaldson was one of those war contradictions: we had him down as being on one side when, in fact, he was on another—or was he on both? In December 2005, just four months before he was murdered, Denis Donaldson made a dramatic public confession. He said that he was a British agent and had been operating as such since the 1980s. Why did he reveal that dangerous secret? Who or what forced him out of the hiding place that was his double life for twenty years? Is there significance in the fact that in 2002 Donaldson was one of those arrested in what became known as the Stormontgate case, a scandal of IRA intelligence-gathering, stolen political correspondence and documents and spying? Of course there is.

The Stormont estate and Parliament Buildings in Belfast is the seat of government in Northern Ireland. It is where the local power-sharing Executive sits and also where the British ministers in the Northern Ireland Office (NIO) carry out their business. Donaldson worked at Parliament Buildings, serving as Assembly group administrator for Sinn Féin. In 2002 the Special Branch and MI5 believed they had uncovered an IRA intelligence-gathering operation in the highest offices of government in Northern Ireland. This was espionage. The incriminating documents were found in Donaldson's home. It set off an earthquake within the political process and that power-sharing Executive constructed so patiently out of the Good Friday Agreement was rocked and destroyed by the scandal. However, long before Donaldson was arrested, along with several others, a lengthy surveillance operation had been underway, codenamed Torsion. There was another informer. By the time the documents reached Donaldson's home, the Special Branch and MI5 already knew everything because they had been watching and listening for months. In this particular operation, Donaldson was not their source. It was someone else. The information I have about Operation Torsion could identify the informer who alerted the Special Branch to Stormontgate. Denis Donaldson was at the end of the line; someone else was at the start.

Republicans do not like this version of events because it does not fit with their script. They prefer to present Stormontgate as a different kind of scandal, something concocted by the 'securocrats'. Their interpretation is that MI5 and Special Branch were involved in an elaborate plot to pull down a government in which Sinn Féin was sharing power with unionists. Chief Constable Sir Hugh Orde, speaking in an interview for this book in September 2007, dismissed that suggestion out of hand: 'If only we were that good. The notion that we are that sophisticated and that organised and could plan that sort of event in that sort of way is such crazy stuff. It is laughable.'

Republicans present the story this way: Denis Donaldson was a British agent; he had the documents. It all adds up. In fact, it does not add up. Let me present another possibility: is it possible that Donaldson had been uncovered as an agent prior to his confession? Was this something republicans already knew? Could he have been outed to support their version of the Stormontgate story? It is a possibility that is, at the very least, worth thinking about.

Donaldson had kept his true role hidden for more than twenty years, and then he broke his silence. In December 2005 the Stormontgate case had just collapsed after three long years in court. The case was not taken to the end of its legal line; charges were withdrawn. Behind the public scenes of this case lay a hidden, protected world. Three men walked free, including Denis Donaldson and his son-in-law Ciaran Kearney. It was just after this that Donaldson made his remarkable public confession. Was he, as we are led to believe, a broken man with a dark secret he felt compelled to reveal? I, for one, do not believe that, cannot accept it. There was an arrogance about Denis Donaldson, a smugness, with no hint or visible sign of any stress or pressure. Here was a man who had played the most dangerous war game and survived for two decades. He approached me a number of times after he was charged in the Stormontgate scandal and around the same time it was reported that his defence team could subpoena me if the cases went to trial. Why? Because I was the journalist who broke the story of Operation Torsion—the intelligence operation linked to Stormontgate.

Whatever else he told the Special Branch and the Security Services in his role as agent, Donaldson did not tell them about Stormontgate, not even when the documents arrived in his house. He could not betray the man who brought them to his home. At no time did Donaldson ever suggest that he was involved in an intelligence-gathering operation inside government buildings. Nonetheless, he ended up in possession of the Stormontgate documents and following his confession, republicans linked him to a securocrat plot. It was an easy explanation because it fitted perfectly with their storyline. Somewhere in all of this Donaldson was compromised, sacrificed and later killed. It was an instance of the war spilling into the peacetime, and it happened after the IRA had put its weapons beyond use. Regardless of processes and politics, somebody wanted Denis Donaldson dead, and there was a gun to do it.

In spite of what Donaldson said, Stormontgate was neither a scam nor a fiction. It really happened. The story behind the story involves a complex web of manoeuvres and counter-manoeuvres, of informers and of secret surveillance by Special Branch and MI5.

There was a 'safe house' in west Belfast, which was the home of Mr X. This house was the hiding place for the stolen Stormontgate papers, comprising a batch of political documents and correspondence. These had been removed from government offices at Stormont and elsewhere in an IRA intelligence-gathering operation and lodged in the safe house. However, what Mr X did not know was that he was being watched and sometimes followed, that he had 'babysitters' from inside the world of secret intelligence. They were very close to him, at times beside him, but he did not see them for who they were. The stolen papers were in his house, and the Special Branch had the key to his front door. I know Mr X's name. An informer—but not Donaldson—had identified the house.

This is where Operation Torsion came into play. It was a Special Branch undercover surveillance operation. I came to know about it, and about how the home of Mr X had been compromised by one of his friends who had become an informer. I learned that Special Branch were in and out of that house, that they took the Stormontgate papers away, photocopied them and put them back in again, that they placed bugs in the house and that they believed all of these manoeuvrings would come together in some grand plan.

At base, Torsion was about trying to trap the IRA's Director of Intelligence. It failed. It was a costly failure not just in terms of financial outlay but in its political and policing ramifications. Donaldson knew none of this. He did not become part of the story until the documents were moved to his home and he was arrested shortly thereafter. This high-level IRA intelligence-gathering operation had in fact been compromised months before the bag of documents was taken to Donaldson's home. I have been told who delivered the bag to his house; the Special Branch and MI5 know who took it there. The security services know the when and how of all this. But Donaldson was not the one who told them. He couldn't have told them because for months he wasn't in the loop.

At one stage in the legal process that followed, Donaldson's solicitor stated publicly that I could be subpoenaed if the cases proceeded to trial. His defence team had not known about Torsion before I reported its detail, which gave rise to a legal battle for disclosure. That was why the case eventually collapsed—because the Special Branch and MI5 had too much to hide. My reporting of Torsion had already revealed too much that was intended to remain hidden. The legal teams representing Donaldson and his co-accused employed the disclosure process in an attempt to confirm the information I had reported. It was a fruitless exercise: Torsion and its wealth of secret intelligence detail was never going to be revealed in a courtroom. It was inevitable that the case would collapse. There would be no disclosure because there could be no disclosure. The identity of the real informer—the close friend of Mr X—has never yet been revealed. There are plenty of clues as to his identity, however, and I feel that if the IRA really wanted to, they could have pieced together the jigsaw long before now. Instead, we got the Donaldson confession and then, just a few months later, his murder. He was no lowly foot-soldier either. This was a man who was at the roots of the modern-day IRA in Belfast, a man who had spent time in jail with Bobby Sands and was a significant figure in the middle tier of Sinn Féin. This was a man republicans trusted; for years they chatted openly in his company.

As a result of this hidden war game, Northern Ireland's power-sharing Executive collapsed. Unionists were no longer prepared to sit in government with Sinn Féin. The IRA stood accused of political spying and in this developing drama the Secretary of State, John Reid, said that the Northern Ireland Office had been penetrated. In October 2002 the Executive was suspended. MI5 was convinced my reporting of Torsion resulted

from a breach of the Official Secrets Act. When it all blew up in
those late months of 2002, Hugh Orde was the man sitting in
the Chief Constable's chair and faced with the job of sorting
through the claims and counter-claims.

What, then, is the truth behind this extraordinary episode in
the Troubles? I can give the story of Stormontgate and Operation
Torsion as I know it, as given to me from sources inside the
intelligence world. In hindsight, Torsion was an operation that
was probably too ambitious in terms of its target. In its failure,
it created serious repercussions: the details of a secret intelligence operation were made public; the most senior Special
Branch officer in the Belfast region, Bill Lowry, was removed
from his post and retired earlier than expected; Northern
Ireland's devolved government was undermined and then
destroyed; and finally the subsequent court case collapsed. One
informer—the unidentified man at the heart of this case—is
still alive; another informer—Denis Donaldson—is dead.
Torsion was about revenge, but it ended in recrimination, with
a fall-out that affected the worlds of policing and the security
services. People had been 'too clever' was the after-the-fact
observation of one senior police officer who was not involved at
the time, but who now knows the case: 'You can let these things
run too long.'

In this case, 'too long' was a period of some months. The
intelligence and security personnel monitoring Mr X's house
knew about the stolen documents, but they did not move in.
That was because they wanted a larger prize. One man, in particular, was their primary target. He was an IRA man who had
long occupied their thoughts and their plans. Throughout the
war, his was a name you would have heard often. You will find
him in the IRA escape from the Maze Prison in 1983 and in the
intelligence assessments of many of the so-called spectaculars
linked to that organisation since, such as the British Army
Headquarters bombing at Thiepval in Lisburn, the Northern

Bank robbery and the raid on Special Branch offices at Castlereagh, in Belfast. His name kept cropping up, but for a system that knew so much about him after the event, it seemed to know very little beforehand. Operation Torsion was about getting this man: Bobby Storey. The officers assigned to Torsion were waiting patiently for him to show up at Mr X's home, but he never did. Then, months later, the documents were moved from Mr X's house to Donaldson's home, creating a dilemma for Special Branch. Donaldson did not tell them he now had the documents because to do so would have been to implicate and betray someone very close to him, too close to be sacrificed to Special Branch and MI5. Donaldson was caught between a rock and a hard place. Had Special Branch moved in earlier, none of this would have ended up at Donaldson's door. But they were so focused on their primary target they blinded themselves to everything, and everyone, else.

Operation Torsion was initiated after a meeting in Grosvenor Road police station. Mr X's friend who went to see the Special Branch that day had some documents to show them—a sample of what was to become known as the Stormontgate papers. He had taken them from a bag stashed under a bed in the safe house. This man bore a grudge: he had had a row with a senior republican over money—thousands of pounds. In the account I have been given, he became an 'eyes and ears' for the Special Branch, i.e. a registered covert human intelligence source. In that very first meeting he gave them so much—not just a sample of the stolen documents but the address of the house where the rest of the papers were being hidden. Mr X's home, treated as a safe house by republicans—was now wide open to a full-scale surveillance operation. That's exactly what was mounted after Northern Ireland Secretary of State John Reid approved the covert methodology of Torsion, which would be a joint Special Branch–MI5 operation.

The timing of all this is significant: it came not long after the

IRA had been linked to a robbery at the offices of the Special Branch at Castlereagh, in Belfast. Bobby Storey was among a number of republicans arrested and subsequently released without charge. The robbery took place on 17 March 2002. At first, it was widely believed to have been an inside job. Within a fortnight, that assessment had been overturned and the IRA was in the frame. This is when Bobby Storey was arrested and held for a short time. The Special Branch believed him to be the IRA's Director of Intelligence and further that, with inside help, it was he who had masterminded the robbery on its own offices. It was a desire for revenge that led them to wait for 'too long' outside Mr X's home, and during that wait they lost everything.

On Friday, 8 November 2002 I met Chief Superintendent Bill Lowry, a senior Special Branch officer, in a coffee shop in my home town of Holywood. By the time I met him I was preparing to run the background story on Stormontgate. I knew that there had been an informer, that there had been a surveillance operation and that the Special Branch and MI5 knew about the stolen documents long before the police seized them and arrested Donaldson. There was something I did not know, however, and Lowry gave me that missing piece: the codename Torsion. Unknown to me, the Special Branch officer then reported our meeting to one of his senior colleagues at Police Headquarters. Within weeks, Lowry was removed from his post and was at the centre of a leaks investigation.

It took me a few days to secure a meeting with Bill Lowry and to find out exactly what had happened. In that interim, one of my senior journalist colleagues in Belfast, Deric Henderson of the Press Association, asked me how I was feeling, 'personally and professionally'. In a straight but gentle way he asked me what I was already asking myself: had I burned a source and cost him his job?

This new situation came on the back of months of build-up. In the period following the Castlereagh robbery I knew my reporting was attracting the attention of those who operate in the intelligence world. Indeed, in September 2002 I was warned by a contact within the police force that my phone could 'be on'. It is a phrase that means the intelligence world is eavesdropping— listening to both incoming and outgoing calls. I am not sure if my phone ever was 'on', but during this time I was drawn into the world of secrets that, while I knew it existed, had been com- pletely closed to me until then. What I would learn was that my report on Torsion was one leak too many for MI5, which wanted this sorted out. Chief Constable Hugh Orde was coming under pressure to conduct a leaks investigation because this was a hole that MI5 wanted plugged, and fast.

I want to describe what was happening on the wider scene at that time. Politically, David Trimble was at his most vulnerable. He had taken his party into the power-sharing Executive with Sinn Féin in the belief that decommissioning would happen almost immediately as a *quid pro quo;* it did not. Security assess- ments were reporting that the IRA was continuing to develop weaponry in the dense jungles of Colombia, that it was behind the robbery of Special Branch at Castlereagh and that it was also involved in the Stormontgate intelligence-gathering scandal. Given all this behind-the-scenes activity, the front-of-house political process was being drained of all credibility, until it finally buckled under the pressure. I have never, before or since, encountered a more difficult or challenging reporting period.

It was a time of hard talking, of questioning and trying to find the truth in two very different stories: a security assessment that was knitting the IRA into the above-mentioned activities versus a republican denial that was spoken and written in the words of 'P. O'Neill'. One had to make a judgment about whom to believe. Choosing the side of the intelligence assessment meant being treated as a 'securocrat', as being anti-peace process, which in turn brought the wrath of the republicans. The IRA closed down my line of communication to P. O'Neill and Sinn Féin joined in a kind of cold war offensive. All of this, I knew, was about trying to force me away from Colombia, Castlereagh and Stormontgate. It was about trying to make me look the other way.

If I was ever to get to the truth of the matter, I knew I would have to find a way into that hidden, secret world that had been closed to me. I found there was a continual political tendency to play down the various crises, a leaning towards damage limitation. The primary focus was to protect the peace process, but all that was happening in this period made that, eventually, no longer possible. Colombia, Castlereagh, Stormontgate and the IRA's involvement in all three was something that was too obvious to ignore or to hide.

It wasn't always so. After the Castlereagh robbery, the initial security and intelligence assessment pointed to an inside job of some description. The break-in occurred on Sunday night, 17 March 2002—St Patrick's Day. At 8.00am the following morning a meeting was convened in the office of Chief Constable Sir Ronnie Flanagan. A senior Special Branch officer was also present, along with two representatives from MI5, including the Director and the Co-ordinator of Intelligence in Northern Ireland. I am told you could feel the tension in the room as the Chief Constable demanded to know: 'Who did it?' Whoever was responsible had to have known the Castlereagh building well, the location of the office known as Room Two-Twenty and the fact that it had only recently been relocated because of renovation work at the police complex. Therefore, from inside and outside Special Branch the initial assessment was the same: an inside job. One senior officer I spoke to on 18 March said those involved had 'an amazing degree of knowledge' about systems and locations, that the robbery had been 'meticulously executed'. It had not been a 'fishing expedition'— 'I don't know the full damage yet [but] it looks serious.'

I could hear that sentiment expressed in everything I was being told—not just in this assessment from someone outside the Special Branch system but also from those inside the department. 'I am personally convinced we have a problem,' I was told by one source. So, was this internal—an insider problem? 'Oh absolutely,' came the response. At this early stage, all of the thinking that was spoken aloud was 'leaning in that direction'. The underlying belief was: 'They [the IRA] could not do it.'

Indeed, what I was hearing was that it would 'be better if it was internal' because of the information that had been taken, because of the implications for the political process if it had been carried out by the IRA. When details eventually emerged of what had been stolen, I could easily understand the panic: agent codenames, handlers' names, an alphabetical list of Special Branch officers and their telephone numbers, plus the log of 'addresses of interest', which comprised a list of the homes of many republicans and loyalists. Early on 19 March a former police detective used one sentence to explain the significance of Room Two-Twenty to me: 'If you are an SB tout, you ring into Two-Twenty.'

So in the initial stages of this investigation there was a consistent assessment that pointed to an inside job. It was, the authorities believed, the only possibility because those responsible were too well informed about the layout of the building, its security systems and the fact that the office had only just been moved for it to be anything else.

And yet it *was* the IRA. They had gotten deep inside the Special Branch's own private offices. Within thirteen days of the robbery the initial security assessment had been turned upside-down. Suddenly the picture changed: the IRA had a man on the inside, someone who knew all about the complexities of the Castlereagh geography, who knew that Room Two-Twenty was manned around the clock, that the office was part of the Special Branch operation and where its new location was in March 2002. The 'inside job' had now become 'an act of war'. The ground under the political process began to crumble, and there were even more sticks with which to beat Trimble.

So, how did this become a story about the IRA? The link, it seemed, was a man named Larry Zaitschek, an American chef who worked at Castlereagh and was in the complex on the day of the robbery, using the gym. At the time of writing, detectives in Belfast are still seeking his extradition from the United States, where he went to live soon after the robbery. His name cropped up in relation to the break-in when the investigating detectives checked his background and found links to republicans; his wedding guest list and photographs were a giveaway. The key component of this investigation was an analysis of mobile telephone contact during the period of the robbery. Calls from a number of phones—purchased using false details—came to light on several nights, including the night of the robbery. A mistake by Zaitschek is what led the police to this network of phones. The chef was using two phones: one bought in his own name, the other bought using someone else's name and address. According to a police source, one phone was for 'his own use, and one for another purpose', that being to contact those in the IRA who were planning the Castlereagh raid.

'He fucks up,' a senior police source told me, 'makes a call to the network from his own phone rather than the clean phone.'

Detectives also discovered that Zaitschek had placed calls to telephone boxes in west Belfast. In a meeting with a police source on 16 April 2002, about a month after the raid, I was told that the mobile phones had not been heard or used since the night of the robbery. The Special Branch knows what happened to them. They were chopped up and dumped down a drain in a street in west Belfast. I was told the location of the dump site, but was also told that investigators had been instructed not to try to retrieve those phones because to do so would compromise a 'source'. This means, of course, that there is the suggestion of another informer.

There was considerable concern within police ranks that I had this information, and I started to hear rumours of a leaks inquiry. A report I ran on 19 April added to that concern. Raids by police in republican areas of Belfast after the Castlereagh robbery produced evidence that the IRA was still updating its intelligence bank. Among the information found were details on Conservative politicians; they had not yet been informed of this. On the eve of my report Secretary of State John Reid phoned the Conservative party's Northern Ireland spokesman, Quentin Davies, to advise him of the find. (Davies' details were not included among those discovered.) Watching the political process, it was obvious that the crisis was building. My report appeared on a Friday, and by Monday the Conservative leader, Iain Duncan Smith, had met Tony Blair, while David Trimble had met the Assistant Chief Constable Alan McQuillan and had requested a meeting with Gerry Adams. During the weekend the IRA again denied any involvement in the Castlereagh robbery and re-stated that it 'posed no threat to the peace process'. In my notes on Monday, 22 April I logged the following comment from a senior republican:

There are people in the Brit system trying to create a crisis. There is a view that you are being used.

This was, I suppose, my warning before the republican chill. A few days later loyalist politician David Ervine put it differently in a conversation with me: 'The securocrats might be throwing crap, but they didn't make it.' Ervine, like many others, was now convinced that the IRA had been involved in Castlereagh. In an earlier note I had logged a conversation with him after he had met John Reid. He told me Reid's biggest fear was, 'do they [the IRA] know what they have?' 'If you can think huge, massive and vast,' Ervine said, 'that's an indication of what's gone [missing].'

One further thing before I move on from this point. In May 2006 Martin McGuinness was named in an Irish tabloid newspaper as a 'British Spy'. Using several of the sources I had spoken

to in the period of Castlereagh and Stormontgate, I wrote a
number of articles dismissing that claim. There was no suggestion from republicans then of me 'being used' by the securocrats.

I found this whole notion of 'being used' insulting. The information I was gathering was adding up to IRA involvement in
Castlereagh. There were convincing arguments and a trail of
information that was leading straight into the republican community. I was checking and double-checking, turning sources
inside out, testing everything I was being told with others. It was
never a case of just getting a piece of information and using it.

Also, when you look back on that period from where we are
today, it all makes sense. The war was not over, not yet. The
British were still at it—bugging, listening, watching and keeping their intelligence bank updated. The means of Castlereagh
and Stormontgate allowed the IRA to achieve the same end. The
two sides were still fighting each other, but in a different way.
They remained in a state of readiness for battle, should that
eventuality arise. It was this that was destroying the political
process and destroying Trimble. The information I was getting
was coming out of the security and intelligence communities.
The Special Branch and MI5 were fully aware of all that was going
on, all that their enemy was still involved in. They were not going
to hide that information in order to aid the development of a
peace process. It was going to be brought to light, and the IRA,
Adams and McGuinness were never going to be able to produce
convincing arguments to counter it. Yes, the 'securocrats' were
behind the briefings, but go back to the point made by David
Ervine: 'The securocrats might be throwing the crap, but they
didn't make it.' The IRA gave them all they needed to throw.

It was during this period—April 2002—that the issue of the
arrests of three republicans in Colombia in August 2001 reap-
peared on the political radar. Gerry Adams declined an invita-
tion to attend a Congressional Hearing in the United States set
up to explore republican involvement in Colombia. The IRA

also spoke on the issue in a telephone contact with me on 24 April. I was on a golf course at the time and scribbled down a statement onto two scorecards as dictated to me by P. O'Neill. It read as follows:

In recent days the issue of the arrest of three Irish men in Colombia has been used again in an intense way by opponents of the peace process in Ireland and Britain in an attempt to undermine and subvert the democratic peace process.

This is a very serious matter indeed.

We therefore feel compelled to respond and to reiterate our position on this matter.

We wish to make it clear that:

- The Army Council sent no one to Colombia to train or to engage in any military co-operation with any group;
- The IRA has not interfered in the internal affairs of Colombia and will not do so;
- The IRA is fully committed to a successful outcome of the Irish peace process. The threat to that process does not come from the IRA.

P. O'Neill

It was my investigation into the Colombian link in this specific period that brought about a breakdown in my relations with both the IRA and Sinn Féin. In May I put a series of questions to the Special Branch through official police channels; Bill Lowry was not involved. Written answers were dictated to me on Friday, 24 May. I want to give a flavour of what I was told and let the reader see this information alongside the IRA denial:

PIRA have been using Colombia as a training ground to carry out tests with their engineering department as they are no

longer able to use the Irish Republic due to the current political climate. It also allowed them free range to explore the
new prototype of devices which they were developing such as
fuel to air devices and rockets.

This, I was told, was 'definitely sanctioned at Army Council' and
the Colombian link was about:

Retaining the ability to manufacture new technology without
the danger of being arrested, and keeping the engineering
department intact and able to function if and when required
if there is any change in the way ahead, or if they decide the
British need a nudge in the right direction.

I used the information in news reports on 13 June 2002, having
spent the period between 24 May and 13 June trying to secure an
interview with the IRA. This was through a conduit whom I
knew was in regular contact with the P. O'Neill of that period.
The IRA's spokesman eventually contacted me just hours before
my report ran. We met, and also had two conversations on the
telephone. Even before these contacts I was aware of the republican mood because I had been left in no doubt. I had been told
by the conduit that 'this [the information I had] would start a
bush fire that could end in an inferno', that I would be 'finished'
with republicans and that I was 'being used'. This last point
was reiterated during my meeting with P. O'Neill in west Belfast
on 13 June.

By now, I knew there was not going to be an IRA interview.
The meeting on 13 June and the subsequent phone contact that
day were simply an attempt to persuade me not to use the information I had. I was read a number of briefing points:

We firmly reject these unsubstantiated allegations about IRA
activity in Colombia, which are made by unnamed securocrats

who have consistently sought to undermine the peace process. We wish to reiterate that the Army Council sent no one to Colombia to train or to engage in any military co-operation with any group. The IRA has not interfered in the internal affairs of Colombia and will not do so.

Those were the official IRA briefing lines, all of which I included in my report on 13 June, but there was more to the conversation than those three sentences. I was told it was 'no exaggeration that our people [the IRA] are fuming' and that there was 'a concerted effort by the securocrats to bring down the peace process'. In no uncertain terms P. O'Neill told me: 'They are using your credibility so that when it goes public [i.e. the briefing I had on Colombia] it has weight.'

Finally, he suggested that what I was about to report could be 'the final nail in the Good Friday Agreement'—emphasising how vulnerable Trimble was at that time—and dismissed the detail of the security briefing I had as 'pure shit'. This is one example of the type of pressure that was being applied at that time. Read what the IRA was saying, then read it against that security briefing. They are two entirely different stories. I now had to make a judgment on which one to believe. The IRA never provided a credible explanation of the role of the three men who were arrested in Colombia, two of whom were identified with that organisation's engineering department, the function of which was weapons development. The balance of truth was with the security briefing and, yes, all of this was driving nails into the political process and into Trimble—but who provided the hammers?

In the past, republicans had demonstrated an ability to defend themselves, to provide convincing arguments when events and information were disputed. An example would be the fallout after the revelations of the secret contacts between the British and Martin McGuinness in 1993. The two sides produced separate accounts of events. In the finest detail, McGuinness and Adams were able to explain the process in a way that was much more believable than the British version. Another example is the debate on decommissioning. The information provided by a range of republican sources over a significant period of time always proved much more reliable than assessments given by British and unionist sources. I had the experience of that contact and of hearing and being persuaded by their arguments. However, there was no such dialogue in the period of Colombia, Castlereagh and Stormontgate. All we got was rhetoric about the securocrats and an accusation about 'being used'. This time, the facts spoke against the republican briefings and as a journalist I spoke against the lines they were producing.

The IRA and Sinn Féin did get back on speaking terms with me, but not for a while. First, I had to endure the freeze-out when I was cold-shouldered by almost everyone. Since then, I have heard republicans quietly hint at IRA involvement in Castlereagh—on one occasion when I was in the company of another journalist. I doubt it will ever be admitted aloud, but the evidence speaks of the IRA being behind that robbery.

In September and October 2002 there were new developments in the Castlereagh case. Information emerged that Larry Zaitschek's ex-wife would be a witness in the police case and was being protected on a witness protection programme. It was suggested that there was forensic evidence linking Larry Zaitschek to the robbery. I was told that this evidence comprised fibres that could be linked to what happened inside Room Two-Twenty on the night of the raid, when a Special Branch officer was overpowered, hooded and gagged. All of this was happening in the background, but it contributed to the build-up of tension that eventually led to the Stormontgate arrests and the collapse of the Northern Ireland Executive.

From Castlereagh, then, we come on to the scandal of

Stormontgate, which unfolded on the morning of Friday, 4 October 2002. David Ervine rang me and I could sense in his voice and tone that something was happening. He told me that the police were searching Sinn Féin's offices at Parliament Buildings. At other locations, arrests had already been made and documents seized. One of those detained at this stage was a former messenger in the NIO, another was Denis Donaldson. He was the Sinn Féin Assembly Group administrator at Parliament Buildings and it was his office that was now being searched. Police vehicles were lined up outside the building and officers in boiler suits were inside. However, for all the show at Parliament Buildings, the detail of the story lay elsewhere. Nothing was found at Stormont, but the style of the police operation proved a distraction and a matter of some considerable controversy. The Speaker of the House, Lord John Alderdice, who was in Canada on a visit to the Parliament there with members of the Assembly Commission, had received no indication in advance that the search was about to take place:

I was wakened up with a message from Parliament Buildings to say that the police were wanting to come in and search … and I also had a call from the Sinn Féin representative who was with us in Canada wanting to know what I was going to do about this and what was happening.

And I must say I was shocked by it for a number of reasons. First of all because when they initially arrived up they did not have a warrant with them … The second thing was there hadn't been any attempt to explore with me as Speaker in advance how they would address the question—if there was a problem, how they would deal with it. And I spoke to some people in the Canadian Parliament about it because, of course, the thing is immediately all over the news. And in the morning I spoke to some people there and they were absolutely shocked and they said if the RCMP (Royal

Canadian Mounted Police) came to the Parliament in Ottawa they would on no account do something of that kind without talking to the Speaker—that there are proper ways of dealing with these kinds of things and that was not the proper way to deal with it. Whatever the security issues, there were other ways of dealing with it … At best it was ham-fisted. There were other ways of doing the thing … but suddenly here, without consultation with me, they were landing up in a frankly not very justifiable way of dealing with things … And, so, we immediately contacted the Chief Constable's office and he said, 'Look as soon as you arrive home I want you to come straight to my office. I want to talk with you about this,' which I did … He was absolutely clear. He didn't stop to say, 'Well now, you know I'll need to find out about this'. He was absolutely clear with me. He apologised, said this was not the proper way for the thing to be handled, and that he was trying to address things. There was no question from his point of view this had not been handled properly and he made that quite clear. In fact it was public knowledge at the time that the Chief Constable had taken that line. So, I think the best that one could say about it was that it was ham-fisted—that it did not deal properly with a legislature, with the proper privileges of a Parliament, and that was nothing to do with whether people had immunity or not. There are proper ways of doing these things and improper ways, and in the end this didn't serve anybody's interests … There clearly was something I think that the police were trying to follow up. I certainly don't take the view that this was purely some kind of absolutely unjustifiable attempt to destabilise the political structures. I don't think that it was that. But I think to some extent what it was, was that local political accountability of the police service had been gone for such a long time that they didn't really know how to behave properly and to treat the political system properly and that that didn't actually serve the interests of security in its proper sense, but actually was disadvantageous to both it and to political stability and political progress. It didn't solve any security problems. In fact, it made them worse.

The *modus operandi* employed at Parliament Buildings and the fact that nothing was found there gave republicans an opportunity to hide the real story of Stormontgate by presenting the whole affair as a securocrat plot and an attack on the peace process. 'They are caught, but they've been able to muddy the waters so successfully,' was the observation of one nationalist political source within days of the arrests.

Alex Attwood, whose SDLP was a senior partner in the power-sharing Executive at that time, believes the police blundered in the way they went about that search at Stormont, 'which was both wrong and allowed the Republican Movement to portray themselves as victim, whereas in truth they were the offender.' Then a member of the Northern Ireland Policing Board, Attwood is convinced that the IRA was involved in intelligence-gathering or spying operations:

I have no doubt for a whole lot of reasons, but it includes that at that time, because of conversations that I was having with senior police, I had a much fuller picture at the time of Stormontgate, of what happened in the preceding nine and ten months in respect of the IRA spying operation ... Whatever information was passed to me, it was passed to me by police under the direction of the new Chief Constable, and therefore the story and the picture that was being painted to me is one that I don't have any doubt about ... Whilst it was quite proper for the police to investigate an alleged criminal conspiracy against the State and against the best interests of the people of the North of Ireland, I have no doubt also that there were some elements within the police who wanted to get the Republican Movement and whose motivations, in my view, were questionable. But the way the whole thing ended up being managed, how the spy ring was exposed, how Stormont was raided, without any doubt gave the Republican Movement advantage when they were in a position of deep weakness. And, therefore, in that way, their responsibility for the collapse of the (political) institutions got obscured because of the way others had managed their responsibilities. I think that the institutions were unstable for a whole lot of reasons, what tipped them over was a spy ring that was exposed in the way that it was, and then clearly managed in an inappropriate manner by elements within the police, and the proof of that was that the Chief Constable was so forthcoming within a day or two of the Stormont raid, in terms of saying that it could have been done differently. But the IRA didn't collapse the institutions. They made their strategic contribution to the collapse, and prior to that because of mismanagement of political difficulties by the leadership of the unionist party it created an atmosphere of mistrust and suspicion to which the Republican Movement and elements within unionism fuelled and contributed to.

On the morning of the search I was told that the real story 'had nothing to do with Stormont, as you will see later today'. In effect, the suggestion was that the search of the Sinn Féin offices was a 'red herring'. Donaldson had been arrested and certain documents found in his home. It was a matter of investigative routine that his office would then be searched. The use of so many police vehicles and officers in boiler suits made it look much more than it was and allowed the search to distract from the real story. In other words, something that was small within the overall context of the police operation was presented as and took on the appearance of being centre-stage. The view of Lord Alderdice that it was at best 'ham-fisted' is an opinion that was,

and is, widely shared. While it will be argued that it was a policing error, the republican description of it as a conspiracy is
something that has stuck in some places. Sinn Féin was able to
create enough doubt in enough minds to turn the story of the
search into a veil to hide the real damage. Behind all the headlines of what happened at Parliament Buildings, an IRA intelligence-gathering operation had been publicly exposed. That was
the story of 4 October 2002. The note I made in my diary that
day reads:

> Police raids north & west Belfast plus SF offices Stormont. Op
> linked to IRA intelligence gathering. Among those arrested
> Denis Donaldson plus former NIO employee at Castle
> Buildings. Reid (the Secretary of State) speaks of "penetration"
> of NIO. Sources call it NIO's Castlereagh. Trimble compares it
> to Watergate.

Those few sentences told nothing of the real drama of that day
and the damage that had been done. I assumed, as did everyone
else observing the events, that the Denis Donaldson who had
been arrested was the republican I had known for many years.
What I did not know then was that Special Branch and MI5
knew him in a different role—as an agent codenamed O'Neill
who had been working for them for years. For some reason,
Donaldson confessed as much in December 2005, one week
after the Stormontgate case collapsed in court. As part of that
confession he said he had met with the Special Branch two days
before his arrest in October 2002. No further detail of that contact was given. I was able to confirm that he did have a
meeting on Wednesday, 2 October. That meeting was initiated
by Special Branch to give Donaldson one final chance to talk.
He was, in the words of an intelligence source, offered 'a get out
of jail card' in exchange for information about the bag the
Special Branch knew was in his house. If he agreed to talk, some

arrangement would be made to allow the documents to be moved from his home before the police moved in to make arrests. A source with knowledge of those events told me: 'He was only met before the raid to give him a chance to come clean. They [the documents] had just moved to him. You want him to come and say, "I've got a load of fucking papers here, and I don't know what to do with them". He didn't open his cheeper.'

This was the dilemma at the heart of the matter: Special Branch was not going to reveal the information it had gleaned through Operation Torsion; Donaldson had to speak, had to tell them what they already knew. That was his only way out of this. But he could not tell them because he could not betray the man who had brought the bag and the documents to his home. The Special Branch and Security Services know who it was. I have been told who it was. And I know why Donaldson did not tell. He was in an impossible situation, a predicament he could not have envisaged when he crossed lines in the dirty war. I did not know he was an agent until he made his public confession in December 2005, but I did know there was an informer at the heart of the Stormontgate case and I also knew that informer was not Donaldson. For months and months the documents had been kept in the home of Mr X. That hiding place was revealed by another informer, not by Donaldson. It was that other informer's information that was the trigger for Operation Torsion.

I am not going to go into the fine detail of who helped me to piece together the picture of the Stormontgate jigsaw. As described earlier, the former Special Branch officer Bill Lowry told me some of the story, but I spoke to others back in 2002 and many times since. It was one of those stories that was revealed over the course of time, bit by bit. The first time I reported on Operation Torsion was on Tuesday, 12 November 2002. Twenty-four hours earlier the police had asked me not to make the broadcast, but I had refused, instead offering them a meeting at the BBC to discuss their concerns. I was in a tangle of information, trying to make sense of it, trying to work out what it all added up to. That first report created turmoil within the policing and intelligence systems, more upheaval, in fact, than I could ever have imagined, and my reports on the secrets of Torsion over a number of years brought about the collapse of the Stormontgate case in court in December 2005.

One consequence of these reports was that the different defence teams had much to pick over and pick at—the bugging and surveillance, the fact that evidence was removed from Mr X's house, photocopied and returned, and the role of an informer in the background. Things that were meant to have remained confidential had been exposed. Within days of my first report on Torsion, Detective Chief Superintendent Bill Lowry had retired; he subsequently claimed he had been forced out of his post. He was warned of disciplinary action regarding undisclosed leaks to the media, an action that was withdrawn when he agreed to retire. Lowry later made a complaint to the Northern Ireland Policing Board, which was referred to the Police Ombudsman. It is in the pages of a confidential report prepared by that office that you get a real sense of the background turmoil.

At the time, I had some indication of what was going on. I have a note, dated 20 November 2002, in which a PSNI source told me: 'This story went off the Richter scale big time. We got steam from up the road [meaning Stormont and MI5]. There are serious concerns about it, very serious concerns.'

In the above conversation I was following up a call in which I had been told that Bill Lowry had been 'effectively thrown out'. I had known nothing of that development prior to receiving that call. Then, almost a year later, in October 2003, a political source allowed me to read the report by the Ombudsman and to take notes. The full extent of the fallout from the Torsion revelations was obvious.

Ombudsman Report

Paragraph 5.1 On November 8 2002, Mr Lowry received a telephone call from the BBC security correspondent, Mr Brian Rowan. Mr Rowan told Mr Lowry that he had a story regarding the Stormont operation which he wanted to "run past" Mr Lowry. Mr Lowry claims that he sought to secure the permission of his supervisor, Assistant Chief Constable McQuillan, but he was not available. He felt that a meeting was required with the reporter and thus he met him.

Paragraph 5.2 Mr Lowry claims that Mr Rowan had sensitive details of the investigation, which were of some concern. Mr Lowry concedes that during the course of this meeting he inadvertently gave the code name of the intelligence operation, which was being conducted, which was sensitive and should not have been divulged. He subsequently reported the meeting to ACC McQuillan.

Paragraph 5.3 The story, which Mr Rowan told Detective Chief Superintendent Lowry he intended broadcasting, was potentially damaging to the ongoing PSNI investigation. High level meetings took place to discuss this and it was decided to hold a PSNI press conference on Monday November 11 2002 in an attempt to distract attention from any news item Mr Rowan might broadcast. That press conference took place, following which Mr Rowan was spoken to by several senior officers, including Mr Lowry, in an attempt to dissuade him from broadcasting the sensitive information that he had.

Paragraph 5.4 Mr Rowan refused to give such an undertaking but offered the opportunity of a meeting with the BBC Head of News and Current Affairs Mr Andrew Colman the next day, Tuesday November 12 2002, to discuss the matter further.

He intended broadcasting his story on the evening of the 12th. It was agreed by ACC McQuillan that Mr Lowry would attend the meeting accompanied by the PSNI Director of Media Services Austin Hunter.

Paragraph 5.5 Mr Lowry explains that his strategy for the meeting was principally to say that he feared for the life of an informant if the story was broadcast. They attended the meeting and Mr Lowry was confident following the meeting that the informant would survive the story. He accepts that he mentioned some sensitive matters in the meeting, which should not have been mentioned ...

Paragraph 5.7 The news item was broadcast that evening and its contents caused concern ...

Paragraph 8.1 Mr Hunter is the Director of Media Services for the PSNI and a highly experienced press officer. He describes the various meetings and press conference. He then describes attending the BBC with Mr Lowry on Tuesday November 12 2002 to see Mr Rowan and the Head of News and Current Affairs Mr Colman. He states that the agreed strategy for the meeting was to persuade the BBC to "pull the plug on the story" as Mr Lowry and others had told him that the life of an informant would be put in serious danger if the broadcast went ahead.

Paragraph 8.2 Mr Hunter describes sensitive information which Mr Lowry unnecessarily provided to the BBC and states that Mr Lowry had confirmed the accuracy of some other sensitive information which the BBC already had. Mr Hunter thought that this was inadvisable. Mr Hunter describes himself as "amazed by what he was telling them". Towards the end of the press meeting he describes how both

Mr Colman and Mr Rowan asked Mr Lowry "if there was a possibility of someone being killed if they ran the story". He describes Mr Lowry's reply as "he could not guarantee it but he was fully relaxed that it was not likely".

Paragraph 8.3 Mr Hunter states: "I couldn't believe what I was hearing as Mr Lowry had no brief to say what he was saying. The whole purpose was to pull the plug on the story." Mr Hunter describes how he tried to retrieve the situation by saying the meeting was off the record, but it was too late. He was concerned by the content of the meeting. He did not immediately speak to the Chief Constable regarding this meeting.

The views and concerns of the most senior detective in Belfast, Detective Chief Superintendent Phil Wright, and the Security Services are also set out in the document:

Paragraph 16.3 Mr Wright states that he informed the Chief Constable that the leaks had been very damaging and the broadcast that week by Mr Brian Rowan was particularly damaging to the investigation. Mr Wright had himself pressed for an investigation into the ongoing leaks.

Paragraph 17.1 … It was confirmed that the Security Service was concerned regarding damaging leaks in the press. The Rowan broadcast on Tuesday November 12 2002 in their view presented prima-facie evidence that a breach of the Official Secrets Act may have taken place.

Paragraph 17.2 On the afternoon of Thursday November 14 2002 a senior representative of the Security Service had a conversation with the Chief Constable in which he said that his organisation would be of the view that an Official Secrets Act breach may have occurred leading to the Rowan broadcast on Tuesday November 12 2002. They recommended an investigation into the issue and suggested that the Metropolitan Police Special Branch would be well placed to conduct such an investigation due to their previous experience ...

Paragraph 17.3 The senior member of the Security Service states that he was paged later in the evening to call the Chief Constable, which he did at 7.15pm. He describes a short conversation in which the Chief Constable told him that the Metropolitan Police Special Branch would be investigating leaks and that Bill Lowry was to be moved to other duties. The conversation was short as a mobile telephone was being used.

Even this précis of the report clearly spells out the inter-police and police–MI5 tensions and the impact of my broadcast of 12 November 2002. Why did I go after the story of Stormontgate? Because I knew there was something more to it than we were being told. I knew that because in a meeting with a senior Special Branch source in July 2002 I had been told they were looking for bugging warrants and the hint was of something of a political nature. When the Stormontgate arrests were made, I just put two and two together. Did I know when I started looking what I was going to find? No. Was my phone 'on' as I went about my work, allowing those in the eavesdropping station to listen? I do not know. What I did know was that the whole case could unravel on the issue of disclosure, and this I knew because I had been told as much in a conversation with an intelligence source in November 2002, some days after the first broadcast about Operation Torsion.

If the defence teams sought disclosure, 'we [the police] would walk away'. That is what I was told and that was how it all ended in December 2005. Of course, it all kicked off again with the startling confession by Denis Donaldson. There had been no indication that this was coming—not the slightest hint. Why confess? Who outed Denis Donaldson? No one has provided a credible answer to that question. There was some suggestion that he was about to be exposed in the media. I do not believe that. No journalist put his or her hand up to claim what would have been a considerable reporting scoop. There has to be some other reason, some other explanation. This is the significant piece of the jigsaw that is still missing.

The sequence of events on 16 December 2005 was a Sinn Féin statement followed by a news conference involving Gerry Adams and Gerry Kelly, and then, separately and in Dublin, Donaldson read his confession to a television camera. As soon as the story broke that day, I said the following in an interview with my BBC colleague Gareth Gordon:

> Well I've heard what republicans are saying today about Denis Donaldson, but my information is that he was not the informer at the heart of the so-called Stormontgate case. My understanding is that the information that Special Branch had on that alleged IRA intelligence-gathering operation inside the Northern Ireland Office came from another source—not from Denis Donaldson, and not from anyone else charged in connection with that case.

It has been suggested to me that Donaldson's role as an informer was compromised in the period between his arrest and the collapse of the case. I have been given an explanation, which I cannot detail here, but the suggestion is that republicans already knew of his agent status, before he confessed privately to them and before his public confession. Is that possible? I do not have the quality of information I would need to answer that question in any definitive way. Several times between his arrest and the collapse of the case Denis Donaldson approached me, wanting to discuss my reports on Torsion, which had formed a significant part of a book I published in 2003. However, I was not prepared to get into any detailed conversation with him because his solicitor had stated publicly an intention to subpoena me if the cases went to trial. In December 2003 Peter Madden was quoted as follows in the *Andersonstown News*:

> In my view we are now in a similar situation to the Bloody Sunday Inquiry, where we have journalists putting inform-ation out into the public domain which is highly relevant to ongoing proceedings. Certainly it is our view that there is information and material relating to Mr Rowan's book that would be crucial for the defence and, for that reason, if these cases proceed to trial, Mr Rowan could well be subpoenaed to attend and give evidence.

Given all we now know about Denis Donaldson, I wonder why he approached me on those occasions. What was he thinking? What was it he wanted me to answer? Did he perhaps think that I believed he was the agent at the heart of Stormontgate? As I wrote earlier, I knew nothing of his agent role before he made that public confession, but I do know he was not the informer who took the Special Branch to Mr X's home and deep into an IRA intelligence-gathering store. For years, Denis Donaldson was everywhere. You would see him wherever something was happening, see him in those places of stand-off and confronta-tion that were linked to disputed Orange marches, see him in the various Sinn Féin offices, including the party's west Belfast headquarters, where he worked after being given bail in the Stormontgate case. It was in those offices that he approached me a number of times, once when I was on the stairway in con-versation with Richard McAuley, a senior aide to Gerry Adams. Donaldson was also important in Sinn Féin election prepara-tions, a member of the team that looked at numbers and trends and helped with assessments. And, wherever he was, we know now that he was listening for the Special Branch and the

Security Services. They were that close, for so long, and yet no one knew. They had pulled off the same manoeuvre in relation to Mr X—training beside him, listening and looking and searching inside his home, but he didn't see them, and he didn't know the role of his friend. The story of Stormontgate and its secrets spilled out—and Donaldson, for some reason, told his secret too. Now he is dead.

His was a humiliating death—lonely, a quiet funeral, no republican oration to remember his early days in the IRA, his days in jail with Bobby Sands, his contribution, his character. When he crossed the line he condemned himself to having to leave Belfast, to the isolation of life in a remote part of Donegal, to eventually being tracked down and found and, finally, to death. What an end for a man who once had such standing and respect within the Republican movement, who had a place in the early history of the modern-day IRA because of his part in the defence of the Short Strand, a vulnerable Catholic community in east Belfast. Yet this is how it has ended for so many—stories never explained properly, truth taken to the grave. His story was no different: Denis Donaldson died with his secrets and was buried with them. No label has ever been attached to his killing because there has been no security assessment that attributes responsibility for that shooting. There remain only questions.

Did it really all go wrong in that one week in 2005, between 8 December and 16 December? Contrast the smiling, confident man of those news interviews, trumpeting the collapse of the Stormontgate case, with the haunted figure just one week later, sitting alone, reading his confession of betrayal. What happened in those few days? The day after his confession a key IRA figure in Belfast described it to me as 'a kick in the balls'. Another republican called it an 'extreme act of betrayal'. Denis, he said, 'is known the length and breadth of the organisation, and he was liked.' It left a bitter taste in the mouths of those who knew him, worked with him, liked him, but who had now come to understand that all they had shared with him they had unwittingly shared with his handlers in Special Branch and the Security Services. But still the central question eludes an answer: did he jump, or was he pushed?

I spent months and months and months working on this story, trying to make sense of it, trying to piece together the clues into a coherent, sensible whole. Denis Donaldson lost his life, Bill Lowry lost his job, the court case collapsed amidst the revelations about Torsion and the power-sharing government was destroyed by the scandal.

Chief Constable Hugh Orde dismisses any suggestion that the police or the securocrats were to blame:

> We didn't cause that. It wasn't the first time that Stormont was dissolved if I remember rightly. Now, hopefully it is the last … The learning of that was, yes, if it was such a big shock [that] people were going to take their time before they got into a [political] system [again] and make sure they had created the conditions where stability was assured, and the biggest disaster in Northern Ireland now [would be] if that thing falls down again. And so it took some time.

It took almost five years to rebuild the Executive out of the ruins of 2002 and the shock of Stormontgate.

So, in spite of the gaps in the knowledge, the infuriating inability to answer all the questions fully, what do I believe about Stormontgate as an investigative journalist? Well, I believe it was a republican intelligence-gathering operation, but in order to understand it one must understand the IRA's journey and that the ceasefire of 1994 was only a beginning, not an end. It is necessary to appreciate that this war finished not all at once in some definitive, dramatic act, but in a lengthy phased and protracted process. For years after the 1994 ceasefire the IRA and the

British had still not made peace, which is why both sides were still engaged in intelligence, bugging and surveillance. These were the continuing war games that, every now and then, spilled into the politics and the peace and interrupted the process. It took years to sort this out, for the republican leadership to move the IRA from the ceasefire to the formal ending of the armed struggle some eleven years later. It was that move plus subsequent developments on IRA guns and the republicans' shift towards policing that helped rebuild the political Executive that was destroyed in the wake of Stormontgate. The next government would be very different.

There is one question from all this that we may now answer. Where is Bobby Storey? The man who fascinated and infuriated the intelligence community in equal measure. The man they were waiting for in Operation Torsion. Bobby Storey is chairman of Sinn Féin in Belfast—surely an indication of how the IRA is fading away and how the political processes are working to achieve a lasting peace.

I watched Bobby Storey and the IRA on the streets of west Belfast in May 2008 at the funeral of Brian Keenan. There were men and women in white shirts and black ties, and a small number wore black berets, but there were no masks and no guns, and this is part of what is different. Storey and Keenan were long recognised as two of the hardest men of the IRA, and yet they were crucial to the peace and to that phase in republican history when Adams and McGuinness changed the orders and direction. Men of the IRA's war became men of the IRA's peace.

Chapter 2

Adams and McGuinness: Changing the orders

I do give Gerry Adams credit for the political nous he showed in subtly step by step bringing this about …
While Adams may not have had as full a military role as McGuinness had … the militarists within the IRA (would have said), 'hold on a minute or two, nobody can question his credentials. So, if McGuinness is for it, let us consider this'. Because he was unquestionably the IRA leader—unquestionably.
(FORMER UVF LEADER GUSTY SPENCE COMMENTING ON HOW ADAMS AND McGUINNESS DELIVERED THE IRA INTO PEACE.)

The genius of them was that they brought an army that was absolutely committed to fighting the British Army in a sense to the last person standing, brought them from that position to a position where they were prepared to call a ceasefire, put their weapons beyond use, and then to call off their armed campaign. That is incredible.
(REPUBLICAN SOURCE COMMENTING ON THE LEADERSHIP OF ADAMS AND McGUINNESS DURING THE PEACE PROCESS.)

There's no question that they have been remarkably shrewd in their handling of the whole process, not necessarily because they were so far-seeing and so clever about planning and so on ... I think they were nimble, I think they were streetwise, they were, in their own terms, courageous. That's very impressive. Now, of course, what will be very interesting is how far they are able to survive, individually or together, in a new dispensation when a completely different set of rules applies.

(FORMER SPEAKER OF THE NORTHERN IRELAND ASSEMBLY AND INDEPENDENT MONITORING COMMISSION MEMBER LORD ALDERDICE COMMENTING ON HOW ADAMS AND McGUINNESS MANAGED THE REPUBLICAN MOVEMENT OUT OF WAR AND INTO THE PEACE PROCESS.)

I believe that the single most important person in this process from the very beginning is the leader of Sinn Féin, Gerry Adams. I'm not saying that because I'm his friend or because I'm loyal to him or anything like that. I think there is no doubt whatsoever that none of this would have happened without the leadership shown by himself—his relationship with John Hume, his relationship with Father Alec Reid. But of all the people in the process that had to shoulder the greatest burden, it was he.

(MARTIN McGUINNESS DEFINING THE ROLE OF GERRY ADAMS WITHIN THE PEACE PROCESS.)

Gerry Adams and Martin McGuinness were part of the war. They were members of an Army Council, a leadership, that gave orders and mapped out direction. But as that war edged closer to peace, those orders changed. Adams and McGuinness took the IRA along a new route. There was some resistance, of course, and at one point an attempt to undermine and overthrow their leadership, but all of that failed. These two men have made the IRA part of the political peace process.

The longest of wars has now ended. It is over, and one of the achievements of the peace has been the forging of a quite remarkable political arrangement—a deal between Paisley and the Provos. The peace after the war has changed both sides, a change that has permitted a once-unthinkable working relationship to exist. The changes took time, though. Consider, for a moment, what the IRA was thinking during the 1980s when its bunkers were filled with weaponry supplied by Libya. Consider the ambitions for what all that Semtex, the rocket launchers, the rifles and all the other bits and pieces of its war chest could achieve. The Army Council must have been thinking: Victory. It certainly would not have been contemplating defeat. We know what the British were thinking in that same period because we can read it in the analysis of the Army's Operation Banner: 'The British Government's main military objective in the 1980s was the destruction of PIRA, rather than resolving the conflict.'

Now consider some of the trends prevalent in those battles of the 1980s. The pendulum swung many times through the events of the republican hunger strikes, the attack on the Conservative party conference in Brighton, the bombs of 1988 that killed so many soldiers in Lisburn and Ballygawley and then, in 1989, at the barracks at Deal, in Kent. As that pendulum moved the other way, we saw the ambushes involving the SAS in Loughgall, Gibraltar and elsewhere, in which the IRA sustained heavy losses. At different times, each side may have thought it was winning. They were capable of killing each other, capable of getting behind each other's lines, capable of spectacular head-line moments. But these were all battles won or lost—not the war itself. It could have gone on like that forever, with one side scoring one day and the other the next day. It was, to all intents and purposes, a stalemate.

This was why Adams and McGuinness needed a context in which to change the orders, because change had become necessary. As that context was slowly created, they had to make an argument inside their army and win over those who still wanted to fight. In the way the IRA works, this was the business of the Army Council, the stuff of debates in Army Conventions, and slowly, the organisation was talked round. When the time was right, the leadership orders were given—the significant first order being the 'complete cessation of military operations', issued in August 1994. Other directives would follow, each con-tributing to expand the space needed for the negotiations and the political work to be done. As they say in Ireland, peace came dropping slow.

Now, we have an excellent vantage-point on all this: it is easier to understand now what was happening then. At the time, during the 1980s and early 1990s, some of the information was hidden in the all-important back-channel contact between the British and Martin McGuinness, maintained via Brendan Duddy and the Security Services, and also in the private dia-logue that continued between Gerry Adams and John Hume.

The two processes were very different. The Hume–Adams interface was a complex political dialogue concerned with how to settle relationships within Northern Ireland, between the two parts of the island and between Britain and Ireland. It was an examination of rights and entitlements, of self-determination, of the British in Ireland, or the 'occupation' as republicans described it, and the denial of rights stemming therefrom. The political discussion begun by John Hume continued into the wider negotiations that would lead to the Good Friday Agreement of 1998. Since then there have been subsequent bouts of political sparring and deal-making, making additions to and subtractions from previous agreements. However, Hume's crucial contribution in that period of the 1980s–90s was his willingness to engage with Adams, to argue and debate with him, even as others demonised and shunned him. Hume's emphasis remained fixed on the weight of argument and per-suasion rather than on the way of condemnation and isolation. We can see now that he was right: there was an alternative to the IRA's war; there was a way of negotiating and working things out though discussion and debate; the endgame had to be a political, rather than a military, outcome. Hume knew this was never going to be settled on any battlefield and that the place of its end would be in a negotiating process that involved and respected all sides. That was his vision, and his significant con-tribution. It is apparent in the Good Friday Agreement and in political deals made since. The Hume–Adams dialogue was, therefore, a critical juncture that became the cornerstone of the peace process.

The other process was the link created between McGuinness and the British Government. This depended for its existence on the back channel that was manned and maintained by Brendan Duddy, Denis Bradley and Noel Gallagher. The public first learned of that back channel in the drama and controversy of 1993 that surrounded a claim by Northern Secretary Sir Patrick Mayhew about a message, purportedly from McGuinness, asking for British advice to end the conflict. It is now widely accepted that McGuinness sent no such message. This episode revealed the lines of communication running from Derry to London. Between the British Security Services and the republi-can leadership were the men trusted by both sides to relay messages and discuss progress, and how progress could be made. Denis Bradley—a former priest now working as part of a consultative group addressing the vexed questions of how best to deal with Northern Ireland's past—has told his story a number of times. The other two men, Duddy and Gallagher, have not. Of the three, Gallagher was probably closest to McGuinness, while Duddy was the link to the British and had been since the early 1970s. In that period, Duddy had been talking to a different republican leadership, the men who would later be replaced by Adams and McGuinness. That process entered an 'ice age' in the Thatcher years, during which the two sides lived in 'igloos'. In the 1980s it had become personal, because of the hunger strikes and the bombing of the Conservative party conference in Brighton in 1984. Nonetheless, all through this time of despair and hatred, Duddy was still talking to the Security and Intelligence Services—'mostly Michael Oatley'.

Duddy described to me his role during this time: 'I was always on the bus. I was never off the bus.' What he means is that even in that stand-off between Thatcher and the IRA, he kept talking to his British links in the chain. The process may have been secret, but Duddy's message was very simple:

> I introduced the word dialogue, and I also used the word process. I was saying to the British, we don't have to live like this, we don't need to live like this. The Provisionals had a black-and-white scenario on everything, and the British were the same.

That had to change. In his conversations with Oatley, Duddy would tell him to 'go and talk sense to that woman'—meaning Thatcher—to which Oatley would reply, 'The time's not right.' This was not Duddy acting on McGuinness' behalf, but acting independently. This has led to some misunderstanding of the function of the back channel, because for a long time we believed it to have been something quite formal and structured—a route along which only agreed messages could pass from one side to the other. It was more than that, however. Duddy spent years telling both sides that there was a different way. He used the back channel for formal communication, but also for dialogue and debate, feeding his own thoughts and thinking. In that hiatus that was the Thatcher years, he kept talking to those he knew on the British side, and by 1990 things began to move again. Thatcher's Northern Ireland Secretary, Peter Brooke, authorised the re-opening of contacts through the back channel, a decision to which Duddy attaches considerable significance: 'It was the British moving forward. They decided to end it on the basis of dialogue.'

If that analysis is correct, then this is the point when the British begin to think about Northern Ireland in terms other than 'winning' and 'losing' and decided on another approach: dialogue. This was about exploring the possibilities of a negotiated political settlement and giving that primacy over any security or military outcome. As Duddy remarks, 'That was the prelude into [John] Major. Thatcher, like McGuinness, was incapable.'

I understand what he means by that. He believed McGuinness incapable of asking for British advice to end the conflict, and Thatcher incapable of negotiating a settlement with republicans. That would have to wait for someone else, and we now know that it went beyond Major, into the Blair years. The Brooke decision of 1990, Duddy believes, was 'the beginnings of movement to re-introduce this situation', meaning re-opening a secret route to the republican leadership, to McGuinness and Adams. They would have to be 're-convinced' that it was worth going back into the tunnel. The republican experience of life in that place in the 1970s and subsequently during the hunger strikes was not a good one. Enemies will always be suspicious of each other—these enemies, in particular. Thatcher had not buckled during the hunger strikes, which is why the IRA had wanted to kill her in Brighton. But now, towards the end of her reign, her Secretary of State was starting to say some interesting things. For example, in November 1989 Peter Brooke said that it was 'difficult to envisage a military defeat of the IRA'. Brooke was rewording the language, reworking the landscape; the thaw had begun.

John Major became British Prime Minister in November 1990, and Patrick Mayhew was appointed Secretary of State to Northern Ireland in April 1992. It was they who would have to answer the questions about the back channel after the journalist Eamonn Mallie revealed its existence in November 1993. Brooke's decision to re-open the link in 1990 had not sent the IRA into any kind of retreat. It had directed its mortar bombs towards Major and his Cabinet in Downing Street in February 1991. Furthermore, when the story of the secret contacts broke the horrors of the Warrington and Shankill bombs were still fresh in people's minds. Two young boys—Jonathan Ball and Tim Parry—were killed in Warrington in March 1993, while that October, in Belfast, nine civilians, men, women and children, lay dead in the rubble of the Shankill, alongside one of the IRA bombers. In response to Mallie's reports about the secret contacts between the two sides, the British government published its version of the back-channel link, including a message attributed to 'the leadership of the Provisional Movement' and dated 22 March 1993. That message related to the Warrington bomb:

> It is with total sadness that we have to accept responsibility for the recent action. The last thing we needed at this sensitive time was what has happened. It is the fate of history that we find ourselves in this position, all we can think of at this time is an old Irish proverb: God's hand works in mysterious ways. Our hope is that this hand will lead to peace and friendship.

In its version, *Setting the Record Straight*, Sinn Féin described that message as 'bogus'. Martin McGuinness had not authorised the message, but it was not bogus—not in the sense of having been concocted by the British. Duddy had sent it because he believed he had to, that it was the right thing to do, because what happened in Warrington was 'completely wrong':

> Warrington exploded in the middle of movement forward and I apologised to them [the British]. It needed to be heard by the other side to allow things to move on. They [the British] needed it, and I gave it to them.

Duddy told me that before sending this message he had tried to contact McGuinness using a third party, and believed he had his approval to make the contact with the British. He had not. The 'movement forward' in the back channel was a momentum apparently leading towards a direct engagement between the British Government and representatives of the republican leadership, based on an unannounced suspension of violence. Duddy realised all of this could be lost in the fallout from the bombs and in the reaction to the deaths of those young boys, but at the same time he also wanted to register his personal disgust: 'There is a point where you say no, and I was saying no. For one of the few times in my life, the process took second place.'

In fact, there was renewed hope within a matter of a few weeks. By 10 May 1993 the IRA had agreed to an undeclared suspension of operations and that message was communicated to the British. Duddy delivered it, after a meeting with McGuinness: 'McGuinness arrived with a one-page—A4— [message], which basically offered what you are saying [agreement on an undeclared suspension of operations].'

It was late at night when he met McGuinness, and Duddy took the first flight to Heathrow the next morning. His thoughts as he travelled were, 'This is it'— a breakthrough.

In a hotel in London he met three representatives of the Security Services: Director and Co-ordinator of Intelligence in

Northern Ireland John Deverell, Duddy's main MI5 contact in this period Robert McLarnon and 'another man', whom he told me he had not seen for six years. Duddy delivered the message as a 'speaking note'. In other words, he read it and it was noted by MI5. Their reaction was immediate: 'They couldn't get out of the room quick enough to report back.'

This all added to his sense that 'this was it'—a decisive moment. The message meant the IRA was prepared—albeit quietly and without public announcement—to create conditions that would allow the talking to begin. However it was done, getting to this point was a major achievement for the back channel. Why? Because it created a new and developing context—a willingness to explore a way out of violence through talks. When two sides agree to enter such a process it does not necessarily mean the conflict is over, but it does mean that it is ending.

For the time being, though, the route the IRA initiative was meant to open up remained blocked. The proposed delegation meetings did not happen and within months the back channel was blown out of its underground tunnel, its debris scattered across the political stage. This is when Mayhew suggested that the whole process was linked to a message received from McGuinness in February 1993 to the effect that the conflict was over, but the republicans needed British advice on how to bring it to a close. It sounded implausible at the time, and nothing has emerged since to make it any more credible. Yet, John Major still uses that alleged message as the reason for the contacts in the back channel.

Denis Bradley has already offered his explanation: the February 1993 message was an analysis provided not by McGuinness but by the back-channel men. It was their argument that the conflict was over and that the two sides needed to talk. Bradley has said he believes someone on the British side added the line about republicans needing advice. It was all about getting the British and McGuinness into a room together, but in the repercussions from the revelations of November 1993, all of this simply added to the mess. Mayhew was almost suggesting that McGuinness and the IRA had surrendered and that all they needed was British help to get them out of the war. That was the interpretation that could be attached to the alleged message. It was why Duddy was asked by Adams to explain this in a four-hour meeting, or 'interrogation'.

Ask Duddy now what he thinks went wrong—why the offer of the undeclared suspension of IRA operations was not accepted, why the delegation meetings did not happen—and you get a one sentence reply: 'The problem for the Major Government was this was going too fast.'

In Parliament, Major needed the unionists, needed them more than this secret process with the Provos. If something was going to be sacrificed it was the process, and it was. As Duddy explains: 'The ground was being prepared [for talks] and then comes, who leaked what and for what reason? Why and in whose interests was it done?'

Although the 'why' of it may be debated, certainly how it was done is something that is known. Mallie's revelations were based on a document provided by the Democratic Unionist MP William McCrea. The questions that arise from this are: who gave McCrea the document and who knew he was getting it?

I don't have the precise date, but some days before the Mallie revelations were published, one of my colleagues at the BBC, David Morgan, drove me to a meeting in Belfast. I do not want to be any more specific than that. Morgan stayed in the car park. Inside, I told the person I was meeting that someone was waiting for me. He seemed concerned, and we went outside and took a walk. Where he was parked, Morgan would not have seen us; it was winter, it was night-time and it was dark. I was told I would be given some information, but not yet. There was a condition attached: once I was given the information, I would attribute it to the DUP. I was not prepared to do that. The whole set-up was very strange and serious, even frightening, in the way it was conducted. It was one of those conversations and meetings that 'hadn't happened', that I should discuss with no one because people could end up in 'body bags'. That is what I was told.

I returned to Morgan's car and told him that we should say nothing about where we had been. I explained that I could not discuss the detail of the meeting with him. He understood. I contacted Eamonn Mallie and we met for coffee close to the BBC's offices. We had been around a lot of corners together, and he knew I was concerned. In confidence, I talked him through what had happened. That night I did not stay at home; that was how concerned I was. There was something not right about that meeting and that conversation, and it unsettled me. This is the first time I have written about it. Eamonn Mallie did his work as an investigative journalist. He was the front-runner on this story of the secret contacts, and from William McCrea he got the document that was the proof of them.

But there still remains my original questions: who gave the document to McCrea and who knew he was getting it? The man I met on that winter's night seemed to know that the DUP had the information, or would have the information. How did he know this? Our meeting took place days before the revelations. Somebody wanted that story out, and I was meant to be part of getting it out. Knowing whom I met, I can guess why he and others wanted the information in the news. I won't name my source, but suffice to say that many hands were at work in the build-up to the blowing of the back channel.

I can still, in my mind's eye, see the awkwardness and nervousness in Mayhew as this story emerged, his unconvincing performance in a Sunday morning news conference and his naming of McGuinness as the author of that disputed February 1993 message. Nobody believed him. The republicans had the more convincing version of events and the documents to support it. The secret links had a history stretching back to the 1970s and this particular phase began in 1990, not 1993. Duddy told me that he had spent weeks in Spain and in the Canary Islands with his main MI5 contact, Robert McLarnon. This was preparing the ground—exploring possibilities, talking, thinking and working through options. And when it all blew out of that political volcano in late 1993, Duddy believed his work had been done: 'The Provisionals had reached the position that everything was in place for movement forward.' He means they were getting ready to talk, and so were the British. It nearly happened in this period, but needed more time to be resolved; it would happen later.

The context that Adams and McGuinness needed in place in order to change the orders was beginning to develop. We can trace it more clearly now than it was possible to trace it then. John Major lacked the political numbers and strength in Parliament to do something bold, i.e. to take the secret process out of its underground tunnel and into a more public place. Nonetheless, I imagine that in the thick MI5 file that charted the work of the back channel could be seen a trend that would have told those receiving the messages that the Provos were getting ready to end their war. The Hume–Adams dialogue and what nearly happened in the back channel were all part of the changing context. Hume had persuaded Adams of a political alternative, and the British were getting ready to negotiate. That was the significance of this period—that the argument in favour of negotiation was beginning to be heard. So much so, in fact, that within months of the fallout in late 1993 the IRA had declared a 'complete cessation of military operations'. This was in August 1994.

The intelligence world was nervous because these were the first steps into a different place and also because, by taking this move, the IRA gained control of the board. It had done something that demanded a considered response. Indeed, this was a different place for us all, something that challenged us to consider a peace beyond war. What did it mean? What had changed? Where was this leading? There were so many questions, but I think in all of the excitement and the euphoria of that moment, we did not want to dwell on the questions and the doubts. We just wanted to enjoy it, to believe it was really over, that from now on things were going to be different, somehow better. I can still hear those whispered words of the woman who was tasked to read the IRA's statement to Eamonn Mallie and myself. We knew a ceasefire was coming, but did not know how it would be couched—what its precise terms would be. It was more than most expected, and it was detailed in those opening words that the woman read to us:

> Recognising the potential of the current situation and in order to enhance the democratic peace process and underline our definitive commitment to its success, the leadership of Oglaigh na h-Eireann have decided that as of midnight, Wednesday August 31st, there will be a complete cessation of military operations. All our units have been instructed accordingly …

Just months earlier I had stood on the Shankill Road in Belfast as people dug in the rubble for bodies after the IRA bomb. Weeks later there had been the revelations of the secret contacts between the British and the republican leadership. On foot of all that, incredibly, there was a ceasefire. We know now, of course, that this was only a beginning, and not the end that many of us thought we were experiencing. But it was a definite step towards the end.

Brendan Duddy had the best seat in the house in terms of reading intentions on the British side. He had all that experience of more than two decades of secret dealings—listening to the British and talking to them through the Security Services. Until very recently, he had lived in that hidden world, unwilling to talk in public about his private role. He is talking now, though, and the information he is giving us helps us better understand the history of this process. Looking back, I think he is right—that everything was moving too quickly for the Conservative Government of that time. John Major did not like the Hume–Adams process, and he became even more concerned when the Irish Taoiseach, Albert Reynolds, got involved in it. The loyalists and the unionists in Northern Ireland feared this 'pan-nationalist approach', as they termed it, and feared it even more when they found out that the British had been communicating secretly with McGuinness. Major could not afford to make any bold political move that would destabilise the unionist community. The parliamentary numbers were not right, the political context was not right, the unionists and the loyalists were not ready for this and the Security Forces and Services had not yet worked out the motivation behind the IRA ceasefire. In my research for this book, I found a note dated 25 August 1994 recording a pre-ceasefire conversation with a senior security official at the NIO, who asked: 'There is a certain naivety about the Provisionals. Look at the current phrase— "time for peace-time to go". What's changed?'

What he meant was that republicans were using different words to say the same thing. It was still about 'Brits Out'. He emphasised the point that the government would move only if there were certainty about a permanent end to the IRA campaign, and in all he was saying to me, I knew he was far from convinced: 'They [the IRA] are also very wary of a permanent ceasefire, both in terms of public opinion and the dynamics of their own organisation.'

This was the source explaining that the IRA was not going to do anything that had the whiff of surrender or the appearance of some kind of military kow-towing to the British. Yes, Adams and McGuinness believed there was a political context in which they could move. Hume–Adams–Reynolds–Clinton and Irish America had helped create a new political mood and new possibilities, but there were prophetic words from the security official at the NIO: 'They [the IRA] are not finished. They really are not.'

He talked to me about the security forces' concerns that the ceasefire was 'being used for the movement of materials and setting up booby traps'. That is how suspicious and unbelieving key people were in this period. There had been too much killing to accept, at face value, the ceasefire of the IRA, which security figures suspected was just another war tactic.

What I have outlined above is the security and political context in which Major and the British paused and tried to wrest control of the board. This would be the beginning of the long debate about decommissioning, which would stretch into the Ahern and Blair years. I am not sure that in that moment of the 1994 ceasefire any of us really knew how the peace would be worked out. We just thought it would be worked out, we expected it to be done. But for the two opposing sides there was much to consider. The terms and conditions of the peace process would take some more years to be written. In that space Adams and McGuinness were fighting internal battles to defend their leadership and their strategy as things moved towards and then beyond the Good Friday Agreement.

As one republican source put it, the process of peace-building meant that 'articles of faith' in relation to republican theology were being challenged. I asked that republican to delineate the challenges faced and overcome in that period, to explain the mind battles as those 'articles of faith' were, I suppose, shattered in the decisions of ceasefire, and then decommissioning, and then, later still, in the republican endorsement of policing. He describes something like a 'counselling service' inside the IRA and across the Republican movement as they were taken on this ideological journey that 'rocked people to their personal and political foundations'. These were the tremors within the IRA, in particular, that had to be managed carefully. There is a view that the dissidents who challenged Adams and McGuinness between the ceasefire and the Good Friday Agreement 'moved too soon', that had they waited, they may well have caught a mood when it came to the issue of the IRA's guns—particularly against a backdrop of limited political progress in the era of Trimble following the Good Friday Agreement.

What is certain is that Adams and McGuinness could not have done this on their own. They needed others to make this possible—political and 'Army' others inside their movement, people in their middle and senior management, people such as Brian Keenan (who died in May 2008), Bobby Storey, Martin Lynch, Sean Murray, Gerry Kelly, Ted Howell, Leo Green, Aidan McAteer, Brendan McFarlane, Padraic Wilson, Thomas Murphy, Brian Gillen, Pat Doherty, Martin Ferris, Seanna Walsh, Raymond McCartney and Richard McAuley. In all of this they needed people who could take the pulse of the Movement and from that judge accurately when to move, and when not to.

An inside source spoke to me about this issue:

I think Brian Keenan's attitude to the whole process was very, very, helpful, because he helped convince a lot of doubters. If it was good enough in a sense for Brian Keenan, then it could be good enough for a lot of people with an IRA background ... He gave leadership. People know this man. They know his history. He was somebody who, at a critical time here, when this city was in flames in 1969–70, he was one of the very few men who rebuilt the IRA from nothing. So, people would listen to him, because they would know that if somebody like Brian Keenan was saying that there are opportunities in this situation (the developing peace process) to advance in a par-ticular way, away from armed struggle, they would listen to people like him. And there are others, who aren't known, who similarly came at this thing from the point of view of giving good quality leadership. But it had to be hands-on, and it had to be almost like a counselling service to provide people with reference points around individuals, who they could talk to and talk through their concerns.

The Keenan argument, I am told, was that republicans were 'morally obliged' to test the alternative, which posited armed struggle was not a principle but a tactic.

The republican leadership was asking for a new way of thinking, for a cessation of previous methods. 'Asking' is the wrong choice of word—the change was ordered from the table of the Army Council. As one source said, 'The IRA is not a debating society':

Obviously the period leading up to '94 and the first IRA ceasefire was a very difficult period for republicans and particularly for IRA republicans—people who spent their entire lives inside the IRA. It was extremely difficult for them. Because they were being asked to face into a reality that they never thought that in their entire lives that they would be asked to face into—namely that the IRA would countenance calling a unilateral ceasefire. And I think that what we have to realise is that the generation of IRA leaders and IRA activists on the ground had grown up in the very firm notion, after the ceasefire of 1974–75 that never again would the IRA ceasefire. So, that was the context—whatever the motivation behind the leadership at the time [of the 74–75 ceasefire], the way it panned out after a few months was, to a lot of people, it was the IRA were being suckered into a situation where they would be defeated. So, this was the very raw mentality that there would have been inside the IRA for the best part of that twenty years [through to 1994] …

So, that was, if you like, the context within which people lived out their lives, went to jail, people died, and then all of a sudden, and that's how a lot of people would have seen it—all of a sudden, because you have to remember this was leadership driven. It wasn't coming from the activists on the ground. This is something, I think, that centred around the Army Council, and obviously the Sinn Féin political leadership among a very small number of them as well. So the whole approach to it was the membership were unaware of the high level of politics that were unfolding, and, so, I would say, even though the Army (IRA) leadership would have done its best in advance of the announcement in '94 to keep their volunteers informed of developments … they were basically telling them [of the ceasefire decision]. There was never any consultation. [What] you have to remember, and it was said to me at the time, is that the IRA is not a debating society. People who join it, join it on the very clear understanding that they're ordered—their lives are ordered and they're ordered in terms of their attitudes, and basically how to think. So, I just think that it rocked people to their personal and political foundations in '94.

We know now that the IRA was maintaining its capacity, keeping its organisation oiled and ready for every eventuality. The bombs in London and then at Thiepval Barracks at Lisburn in 1996 were the violent confirmation that the war was not yet over, that while a political alternative was being explored, it had not yet been developed. A republican offers this viewpoint:

You have to remember that eighteen months after the first IRA ceasefire, the ceasefire broke down, and there was then a resumption of a limited form of armed conflict. And, so, therefore the people who, if you like, manage the IRA, keep the IRA cohesive, they had to ensure that the IRA had a fighting capacity at every stage along the way—the capacity to resume armed struggle in the right circumstances. So, you have to remember that throughout this entire (ceasefire) period the IRA would have been a functioning army, obviously not directly involved in operations, but clearly a functioning army that has the capacity … anybody who knows anything about these type of conflict situations … will know that your army has to be ready … I think the very fact that the ceasefire broke down after eighteen months tells you that there was a commitment in there to go back to armed struggle, and I think myself that that commitment was there at various stages along the line—certainly for the first five to seven years [after the '94 ceasefire]. I think you were into that type of situation where it could have went either way at any time. I think that there's no doubt that Tony Blair coming into office—for example his willingness to talk to Sinn Féin, his willingness to put in place all-party talks, the Good Friday Agreement … that guy came at the thing realistically. He listened to republicans. He listened to people like Gerry Adams. So, I think that Tony Blair's mind was open to the republicans and what the republicans were saying, that they needed to convince their base that this was the right way forward. It had to be a managed process, but it was a very volatile situation for quite a long period of time … And of course [the IRA] also had to deal with the threat of loyalists at the time. That was never far away, and these are the type of contradictions that organisations like the IRA have to cope with. On the one hand, you want to make a commitment to the peace process. On the other hand, they have to defend their volunteers, defend the capacity of the IRA to deal with very difficult situations whether from loyalists or for that matter to resume armed conflict.

In that commentary, what stands out is the assessment of just how volatile things were inside the IRA and for how long—right throughout that period of the mid- to late 1990s and beyond. It was after the collapse of the original ceasefire and in the period leading up to the Good Friday Agreement that some of the most senior figures in the IRA moved against Adams and McGuinness and their strategy. This struggle took place at the highest tier of that organisation, at the level of its Army Council and Army Executive (a kind of watchdog at the very top of the hierarchy), and was driven by senior figures, including the Quartermaster General Micky McKevitt and the Director of Engineering. This was a hidden battle, one that was argued out secretly within the IRA, including inside what that organisation calls its General Army Convention. This was not simply a political tiff of some kind, it was more akin to an attempted military coup—an attempt to seize military control of the direction of the IRA. The Army Council was not destabilised, however, although there were resignations at the level of the Army Executive. A republican source confirms the seriousness of the situation:

> That was a challenge. There was no question about that— that was a challenge to the whole strategy in the Army Council. That was a deliberate attempt (by the dissidents) to take as many Army Council people with them as possible.
>
> I think they (the dissidents) moved too soon and the emotions weren't with them, and also they didn't have a political leader who could articulate exactly their feelings. So, it was very much an in-house schism inside a very senior part of the Army (IRA) leadership. I think by that stage the bulk of the Army's minds were opening up to the process that Gerry Adams and Martin McGuinness were outlining to them. I think a lot of work had been done with army volunteers by that stage to convince them to remain in the organisation.

These are things we did not see at the time; we learned about them afterwards. This internal manoeuvring within the IRA, particularly at its leadership tier, was an issue that had to be

addressed before the organisation could move on to the bigger
questions of political compromise, decommissioning and
policing. And that is what is meant by the dissidents moving
'too soon': had they waited, there may have been a better opportunity for them to catch a mood. Adams and McGuinness knew
they were coming for them, so they, and the Army Council,
allowed an Army Convention in late 1997 because they knew the
dissidents did not have the numbers or the key personnel on
their side and were not organised. As a result, the Adams–
McGuinness leadership survived, along with its strategy for the
future. The dissidents voiced their threat in a number of bomb
attacks just before the Good Friday Agreement, but then they
buried themselves in the Omagh massacre and the bomb of
August 1998. It could have been different—if Keenan, Storey or
Gillen had taken another side. That was something mainstream
republicans always understood—that with a different leader,
the dissidents would have posed a much more serious threat,
both inside the Republican movement and beyond in the developing peace process. It was, according to a source who spoke to
me for this book, something that Gerry Adams recognised:

He said all these people [the dissidents] need is a Brendan
Hughes [a one-time senior IRA leader in Belfast, who died
February 2008]. And you see what that tells you is the volatility of the republican community and the volatility of the
republican mentality—that somebody like a young Brendan
Hughes, who was a capable leader, [capable] of giving directions, of moulding an army, could have easily organised an
alternative. And one of the reasons why, I think, that those
people who left the Army … didn't succeed, in my view, is
they left, they moved too early. Had they moved later … they
could have caught a mood later, because when they moved
there was no sign at that stage of the big changes the Army
[the IRA] had to undergo … They moved at a time whenever

the most the IRA were being asked to do was ceasefire, but later on when the IRA was being asked to do a whole series of different things with their weapons and whatever against the backdrop of no political success or political movement, then would have been the time, I think, to create a much more difficult time for the IRA ... That [the ceasefire] was bad enough for them to have to come to terms with ... Then, whenever other issues, which I would call strictly related IRA matters, came into play such as the whole question of the IRA's guns for example, and if you look at how the leadership handled that, they, and this in my view is the only way that this could be handled, was that it was drawn out over a protracted period of time, and that in order for it to be dealt with with any degree of rationality, there had to be obvious political progress.

For that reason this question of the IRA's weapons was never going to be dealt with in the period of Major's Conservative Government. Later, Blair's bold move and his significant political achievement during his early period in office, when he worked with the new Irish Taoiseach Bertie Ahern, was to create talks even though the issue of decommissioning remained unresolved. Trimble's unionists, John Hume and the SDLP, the representatives of the loyalist organisations, the two governments, President Clinton's representative Senator George Mitchell and Sinn Féin were all inside the negotiating tent, with Paisley, at this stage, on the outside. This was the work that would lead to the Good Friday Agreement, it was, in essence, the politics of power-sharing and negotiating workable agreements on North–South and British–Irish relations. It also brought into the frame of conflict resolution hugely contentious issues, such as prisoner release and police reform. Trimble was unable to manage his party through the period that followed, but Adams, McGuinness and the IRA Army Council held that organisation together, and in the process made the dissidents look small and insignificant. As a republican source says:

> The political process didn't work in terms of delivery for a long, long period of time, and I think that the talks that came out of the Good Friday Agreement, for example the whole business around the release of prisoners, that was a big plus, the commitment to a new police service under Patten [a Commission headed by Chris Patten] was another issue that could be used to try to convince IRA volunteers that the issue of weapons has to be looked at afresh. But none of it was easy, and I was very surprised that we didn't lose more senior volunteers—senior Army [IRA] personnel.
>
> The genius of [Adams and McGuinness] was they brought an army that was absolutely committed to fighting the British Army in a sense to the last person standing—brought them from that position to a position where they were prepared to call a ceasefire, put their weapons beyond use, and, then, to call off their armed campaign … That is incredible … This was leadership driven—Army leadership driven, Sinn Féin leadership driven, but particularly on IRA related matters, the Army Council, I think, have displayed leadership of the highest possible standard, because they gave quality leadership to people who could easily have walked away from them and formed another organisation … What you have to remember in all of this, is that like any kind of army it needs to see people it can trust in the public arena. It needs to see people who—[and] I'm specifically thinking now of people like Martin McGuinness, people like Gerry Kelly, and other people who maybe aren't so well known, that they are prepared to stand up and say, 'I think they are right' [those pushing the alternative strategy to war], and you got a lot of that, you got a lot of senior management people, middle management people, standing up in meetings of Army units

and saying, 'I think what is being offered, what is being suggested here, is the right thing to do'. There was a lot of hidden
advice given to settle people down, who didn't want to go
down that particular road. And there was public advice given
by Gerry Adams in particular and by Martin McGuinness ...
[but] there had to be a private management process because
you're talking about hundreds of volunteers being convinced.
You can't do that on television. You have to sit down with
people. You have to talk them through all their fears and all
their concerns and all their angst, and you have to point them
in the direction that you firmly believe [in].

Back at the beginning of all of this, I don't know how much of
a grand plan Adams and McGuinness would have had in their
heads. Certainly they would not have had the precise detail of
what would happen and when. A lot of this was reaction and
informed guesswork, plus they were always looking at two
distinct pictures: the one inside their movement and the one
outside, in the political process that was developing around
Trimble. I imagine that by the time of the Good Friday
Agreement they would have assessed the dissident threat and
seen the limitations of that threat, both in terms of its potential
to destabilise the IRA and to affect the wider political process. At
the Army Convention in late 1997, Adams and McGuinness won
the fight or the argument at the level of the IRA leadership; they
isolated McKevitt and those around him. Then, of course, the
dissidents destroyed themselves in the Omagh bombing, an
atrocity that was so out of place and out of time in the growing
peace. McKevitt and those with him were not capable of
mounting an alternative IRA war—not then, and not since.
Adams and McGuinness have kept control of the movement.
The story was very different on the unionist side.

Chapter 3
Thinking the unthinkable

If they (the DUP) wanted into government, then they had one big reality to face—that the only way into government was alongside Sinn Féin.
(MARTIN McGUINNESS ON THE INEVITABILITY OF THE DUP THINKING, AND DOING, THE UNTHINKABLE.)

In the description of the republicans' internal process as an IRA 'counselling service', we get a good understanding of just how delicate and how raw much of this was. These were debates in which the heart, the head and the conscience were at war with one another, and it all proved too much for some. However, all of that was managed very effectively and, for the most part, privately through internal housekeeping. The unionist war, on the other hand, was much more public, with its battles involving Trimble and the MPs Jeffrey Donaldson and Martin Smyth, with the old party leader Lord Molyneaux being awkward; others sat on the fence. In those circumstances there could not be a bold republican move, at least not until they were sure of the unionist ground, sure who was in charge.

So, in the same way that the arms question was not going to be resolved in the period of Major's government, nor was it going to be settled during David Trimble's reign as the political leader of unionism. Yes, there was progress, indeed very significant progress—a power-sharing Executive, Martin McGuinness and Bairbre de Brun as Minister for Education and Minister for Health respectively, prisoner releases, a process of police reform and a tentative start to addressing the arms question—but there was also a great deal of uncertainty. This new political beginning challenged the unionist mindset and caused turmoil within that community—Paisley still saying 'No' as loudly as ever and Trimble constantly preoccupied with fighting battles inside his own party, which amounted to his leadership continually being questioned, challenged and undermined. A still 'functioning' IRA added to his problems, especially the questions that arose out of Colombia, Castlereagh and Stormontgate.

It was clear that Trimble was not going to survive—a fact that was becoming increasingly obvious. Paisley took the leading political role in Assembly elections in 2003; Trimble lost his Westminster seat two years later and was succeeded as Ulster Unionist leader by Sir Reg Empey. A party that had dominated Ulster politics for so long inflicted so much damage on itself because of infighting after the Good Friday Agreement that it handed Paisley the opportunity and the ability to walk over and through it.

At base, Trimble did not understand the IRA, and republicans did not understand him. Had they treated each other differently, tried harder to put themselves in each other's shoes, then Paisley's route to power may well have been blocked. But the fact of the matter is that the process now took another path, one that had not been charted on the peace process map. This journey brought the sides to a new place, and to a new deal. It was not a straight road—there were the blind corners of bank robbery and murder, and the cul-de-sacs that were Paisley's language when he spoke of 'sackcloth and ashes' and 'over our dead bodies'. In spite of all the threats, the parties continued along this path, which led to the current state of affairs. However, the roles played by Trimble and by Hume should not be forgotten. Their Nobel Peace Prize was recognition of their roles in ending the war. For his part, Trimble's contribution was to make things significantly easier for Paisley by introducing into unionist minds the political and social realities of life after the fight. He didn't get a chance to see it through to reality; Paisley would win that accolade.

Lord Alderdice, former Speaker of the Assembly, gave a thoughtful overview of the situation during an interview for this book:

> I think they [republicans] pushed Trimble too hard, and in the end they pushed him over the edge. Could that have been different? I think it could have been. Some of it may well have been Trimble's own handling of things—that he's not always maybe the closest to people, and he is a bit impatient sometimes, even with his own party colleagues in the past, and may not therefore have won much sympathy from republicans or indeed others. But then they [republicans] pushed him a long way and the Prime Minister Tony Blair led him a long way ... I think they did over the last year or two almost discount him and almost feel that he was going to go anyway, because it was all getting out of control.

Trimble was never the dominant figure within his party that Adams was, and is, within the Republican movement and that Paisley was within the DUP. Nonetheless, Trimble remains convinced that he got a good deal in the Good Friday Agreement, both politically and on constitutional arrangements. That was only part of the story, however. Those within unionism who opposed the Agreement, and they were many, had numerous sticks with which to beat Trimble—Martin McGuinness in charge of Education, the Shankill bomber being released from jail, the IRA as an organisation still intact and still armed and the Royal Ulster Constabulary about to be thrown to the political wolves. Trimble was set about by his opponents very efficiently, and as we watched him stumble and eventually fall, we began to think the unthinkable: to consider the suddenly real possibility of a deal between Paisley and the Provos. The first time I said it aloud, it sounded so ridiculous—it had failed to work with Trimble, so how could it possibly work with Paisley? In an interview for this book, I asked Martin McGuinness if he had given up on David Trimble by this point:

> Obviously the backdrop to all of this was the changing political landscape … and the elections of 2003 when effectively the Democratic Unionist Party became the predominant force within unionism, and, in my opinion, much of that was the fault of David Trimble.
>
> I was part of a government alongside David Trimble in which there was always a great sense of insecurity, and always a very deep appreciation in my mind that David Trimble was spending more time being fixated by Ian Paisley and the DUP than he was about wrapping his arms around the Good Friday Agreement and getting on with the institutions of government. So, I always felt that we were in a very difficult situation, and in a situation where because of his volatility that Trimble would, at a moment's notice, pull out of government, and mostly because of the ongoing political and electoral battles between himself and the DUP. So, when the political landscape clearly changed, and making an assessment of the state of both parties—the Ulster Unionists and the DUP—it was very clear to me that the Ulster Unionists would never be in a position within the foreseeable future from that moment on to be the predominant force within unionism.

These words confirm the shifting republican focus, which moved away from Trimble and onto the DUP. In this respect, Adams and McGuinness gave up on Trimble before Tony Blair did, as McGuinness admits:

And, of course, you know I had many, along with Gerry, many conversations with Tony Blair in Downing Street about the situation.

Blair was, I think, hoping against hope that circumstances could be created which would see a reversal of that situation … I certainly can say without fear of contradiction that he did believe that the political fortunes of the Ulster Unionists and the DUP could be reversed. And I told him in no uncertain terms that he was living in cloud cuckoo land—that that was not going to happen, and that what he had to do was work on the basis that … the Democratic Unionist Party were the people who needed to be brought to the position of accepting power-sharing, the all-Ireland institutions, and the east-west arrangement—effectively to sign up for the Good Friday Agreement in whatever language they wanted to dress that up in … Therefore our efforts within republicanism were to, on an ongoing basis, contribute to a political scenario which would see the DUP eventually being put in a position where they would have to opt for the Good Friday Agreement.

Perhaps Blair was hoping against hope because, as with so many of the rest of us, it was very difficult to imagine this other scenario, to imagine that Paisley could be brought not only into the politics of power-sharing but into an arrangement with McGuinness. 'That's precisely it,' a source close to Blair confirmed, 'frankly [it was] a desire not to write-off moderate opinion.'

McGuinness was right, however, there was only one realistic route to power and Blair came to recognise that, as the same source reveals:

Immediately after the Assembly election [of 2003] the Prime Minister and Bertie [Ahern] actually met in Wales on the day of the results, and the message was they recognised the mandates of Sinn Féin and the DUP, but with that mandate came responsibility to make devolution work for the people of Northern Ireland.

Both sides said that's what they wanted. The key question was, could they:

- [republicans] find a way through the problems of decommissioning and policing;
- and [the DUP] deliver those in their ranks for whom the thought of power-sharing with the other side was anathema.

Four years after that election, those questions were finally answered.

In the early summer of 2004 I contacted Peter Robinson, (then) Paisley's Deputy Leader in the DUP. I was also speaking regularly to Paisley's son, Ian Junior, and to other senior figures in the party. To have such regular contact with these politicians was new territory for me. My job was to provide a journalistic assessment of possibilities and to make a judgment on what the IRA might do, I needed to know the thinking at the highest level of the DUP. The first thing that struck me was how little the two sides knew about each other and just how far apart they were, even now, a decade or so after the first IRA ceasefire. I had many meetings and many conversations with Robinson that went beyond the usual routine of the journalist asking the questions and the politician answering. Instead, I found I was being asked questions, and not just by Robinson about republicans, but by republicans about the DUP. On air, in my work, I was reporting all the information I was gathering, but I was being asked as many questions outside the confines of the BBC studios as I was being asked inside them. That questioning from all sides told me something: I began to believe that this thing could work, that a deal could be done. Why else would Peter Robinson be spending so much time talking to me and asking so many questions? And why else would the republicans be suddenly so interested in the

DUP? It was starting to become clear that these would be the parties of the new deal—whatever that deal would be and whenever it would be done.

I found Robinson easy to deal with and less prickly than Trimble. Although, to be fair to Trimble, he had never really been able to relax because he was always under intense pressure from those within unionism who wanted him to fail. The DUP was a different party, however, and Paisley, like Adams, was a dominant leader. His people, or the majority of them at least, were going to follow him along whichever road he chose to walk; that was Paisley's huge advantage over Trimble.

The process now became a waiting game for Paisley's decision. In these negotiations he would ask for too much—an indication of how little he knew about republicans. In a much earlier phase of the peace process Adams and McGuinness had refused to surrender the IRA to the demands of John Major and Patrick Mayhew, and there was no way they were going to sacrifice that organisation now to give Paisley his victory. Remember, this was all new to the DUP, and because they refused to negotiate directly with republicans they were depending on second-hand information from the British and from Blair's advisors. The expectations the DUP harboured regarding decommissioning, about who would witness it and about photographic proof, were far too ambitious. I told Robinson as much many times, told him that I had heard nothing on the republican side to suggest the decommissioning process would be photographed. I said it to others on the unionist side, too, but they were hearing something different from the British and, I think, giving more weight to those assessments. I can understand that. After all, the British had comprehensive intelligence information and the advantage of all those meetings with Adams and McGuinness. However, I had the advantage of knowing how wrong the British had been on this issue in a previous negotiation. Now, I watched as this latest phase of talks, stretching through much of 2004, repeated the mistake of expecting and believing developments on decommissioning that were not possible. In my work during those two periods—first, the Trimble period and then the Paisley negotiation of 2004—I spent more time discussing decommissioning with republicans than any other issue. My guidance came from inside the Army Council and, in addition to the organisation's various P. O'Neills, from a key source close to Adams. The issue of how the IRA would deal with its weapons was always going to take time—more time than Trimble had—and it was never going to be done in a way that would meet Paisley's demands. Those were things about which I was certain.

I say 'certain' now as I look back, but in those times I was checking and checking and checking again, repeatedly questioning my sources on the republican side, trying to make sure that the assessment I had was the right one. Progress on the arms issue—or lack thereof—would determine, at various points, whether the process would move forward or stall. Furthermore, on the question of weapons so much was being written and said by others, both in the Trimble era and then as Paisley took over, suggesting much more was possible than I had ever believed, which made it even more difficult to separate actuality from hope. The British were at it, so to speak, hyping up possibilities, talking it up, trying to keep first Trimble on board and then Paisley. Yet, with all their listening gadgetry, one would assume they must have known the republican mind on this matter. Personally, I think they made the mistake of applying political logic to the process, reasoning that if the first Executive were to survive, then the IRA would have to decommission to meet Trimble's needs and that if republicans really wanted a deal with Paisley, they would have to give him his photographs. All these years into the process, yet the British and the unionists had still not come to understand the IRA. That much was obvious. It was why Secretary of State Peter

Mandelson had to suspend the first Executive in February 2000, and it is part of the reason why the first negotiation with Paisley failed in December 2004. Ten years after the 1994 ceasefire the IRA was still doing things its way, as McGuinness describes:

> Let me put it like this, we're nobody's fool, and whenever we go into a negotiation I like to think we do our homework, and we make our own assessments where everybody within that process is coming from.

However, in the negotiation that stretched through the months of 2004, we began to see the IRA's endgame. That new picture began to develop before our eyes. McGuinness again:

> It is our job to try and assess where we think other partici-pants in the process are at, and whether or not, particularly now from that moment on, whether or not we were going to be dealing with a DUP that was going to be at some stage made amenable to the type of political scenario that we have at the moment, and we made the assessment that we could do it—that it was possible to do it. And no matter how ludicrous it may have sounded to the general public, and even many within the media, that we could contrive circumstances which would see the DUP being brought to the negotiating table with Sinn Féin, and the fact is that I have known for a number of years that it was possible to do that—to create those circumstances, and I think the events of May the eighth [2007] have totally vindicated my assessment.

Three years earlier the two sides did not know each other, and a deal then might well have been too soon. This process could not be rushed because there was so little trust and so many suspicions and questions. So, all in all, maybe it was for the best that it took until May 2007 to finally settle things because it gave more time to both sides to make their preparations and get their people ready. What the negotiation of 2004 did provide was a better understanding of where all of this was going. It gave us the detail of what needed to be done, and it told us that the DUP would go into government with McGuinness, if the IRA created the right circumstances.

Ultimately, the 2004 negotiation was lost in the storm of a vociferous Paisley speech and his shouted insistence that republicans needed to wear 'sackcloth and ashes'. He said it as Gerry Adams, Martin McGuinness and Gerry Kelly were preparing for their first meeting with the Chief Constable of the Police Service of Northern Ireland, Sir Hugh Orde, and he said it to emphasise his demand for photographic proof of decommissioning. He wanted the pictures; republicans believed he was trying to humiliate them with such demands. Ian Paisley Junior said something to me in an interview for this book that I think confirms that the 'sackcloth and ashes' moment was about terminating that first long negotiation. He had called me to arrange for a television camera to be sent to the hotel where his father was speaking, and it was the only camera that recorded the speech. Its content confirmed the worst fears of many and fingers were pointed at Paisley Junior, who was seen as the wrecker.

> I wish I'd that power. I don't have that authority, I don't have that power, and my father is too long in the political game to be used like that. He ain't the puppet in anything, and I'm not the string master in anything … and put it like this, a few tough words from the 'Big Man' of unionism wasn't really going to hurt the great Oglaigh na hEireann.

That was Paisley Junior speaking in October 2005, but he said something else to me in an interview for this book, recorded in October 2007. We were discussing the importance of republican support for policing and how crucial it was in the making of the deal of 2007, when he said the following:

Its absence was the reason why you came to a certain hotel, or you sent a camera to a certain hotel in Kells shortly after [the] Leeds [Castle negotiations of 2004]. I mean the absence of the policing deal was why Paisley senior took the view— 'over my dead body'—'sackcloth and ashes'. There has to be something with regards to policing, and policing was just one component Sinn Féin wouldn't even play at at Leeds [Castle]. It took us from Leeds [Castle] to the St Andrews [negotiations], which is two plus years [later], to actually not only get it on the agenda but to make it *the* negotiating point of that process.

Reading between the lines of those comments, I think I can now see why the camera was called to Kells. It was because the Paisleys were not yet ready for a deal and that night, and that speech, were about sending out that message and ensuring it was heard outside the room—by Tony Blair, Bertie Ahern and the republican leadership. It is what I meant earlier about all of this happening too soon. Nonetheless, that negotiation was important because it outlined the contours of the map that would lead the way to the eventual deal, via a convincing end to the IRA's armed campaign, a decommissioning process, an endorsement of policing and, for Paisley, power-sharing and politics with a North–South dimension.

What that map did not show, however, was the volcano that would erupt some weeks later when the IRA was linked to a multi-million-pound bank robbery in Belfast and to the murder of Robert McCartney, also in the city. It was Stormontgate all over again, but this time it was worse. It made it painfully clear that the process was going nowhere, at least not until the questions of the IRA, its activities and its weapons were answered in a conclusive, definite and unequivocal way.

According to intelligence assessments, the Northern Bank robbery was a planned IRA operation that was sanctioned at leadership level and that could not have proceeded without Army Council approval. As such it was very different from the McCartney killing, which started as a pub row and ended in a fatal stabbing. The main suspects in the McCartney attack were IRA members; that has never been disputed. In their campaign for justice, McCartney's sisters and partner made sure everyone knew who had been involved. They laid their brother's death squarely at the door of the IRA, and it could not be brushed aside. At this time it sounded a death knell for the process and unionist–republican relations.

Then, in the middle of all this turmoil, there was a remarkable, almost surreal moment: an offer by the IRA, after courts-martial, to shoot those who were responsible for McCartney's death. It is one of those moments in my reporting career that I will never forget—seated in a small sitting room in a house in the Falls area of Belfast, reading that statement in the company of the IRA's P. O'Neill, seeing the line and thinking to myself: what next? Eamonn Mallie and I sought clarification as to what exactly was being offered, and we were allowed to believe that 'shoot' could mean kill. Bear in mind, this was March 2005, *eleven years* after ceasefire. What the IRA was saying was that it was prepared to shoot those involved in Robert McCartney's killing. That action, that offer would have needed the approval of the Army Council. What were they thinking? What had made them adopt this position? What if the McCartney family had said yes? In that sitting room, on that March afternoon, I could not think or see beyond that startling line in that long statement. Elsewhere, however, others with different jobs to do were already looking on this as a turning point, as Ian Paisley Junior describes:

> The timing of the Northern Bank (robbery) couldn't have been worse for them and couldn't have been better for us ... It played right into our hands.

Those incidents—the McCartney murder and the atrocity of that, and, I suppose, the wave of emotion that [swept] not only across parts of working-class republican Belfast, but also the wave that had [swept] across the Irish-American caucus in America, that was very, very significant and shouldn't be underestimated. The timing of the Northern Bank thing … all of that demonstrated to the rest of the world that when we were saying things like, 'they hadn't crossed the Rubicon, they're not serious about this', it gave those arguments credibility, and I think they were honest arguments. And we very much felt throughout this period that America was more on our side than it was on their side. And I think that was probably the first time in about 25 years of the Irish Question that that actually was the feeling among unionists.

The security assessments linking the IRA organisation to the robbery and its members to the McCartney killing were seen and accepted by the Independent Monitoring Commission (IMC)—a body of four commissioners in a watchdog role—which examined not just the question of ceasefires but the whole gamut of paramilitary and criminal activities, both republican and loyalist.

Lord Alderdice serves as one of the commissioners on the IMC and therefore got to see the intelligence assessments of MI5 and the police forces North and South. As it now stood, the PSNI Chief Constable, the Garda Commissioner, Tony Blair, Bertie Ahern and the IMC all believed that the bank robbery had been a sanctioned IRA action:

After the McCartney murder and the Northern Bank—the IMC comes out with a strong report that is absolutely clear and unequivocal, because we were in a position honestly to do so.

The reaction that that created, especially in the United States of America, was enormous. And the President then said (to Sinn Féin), 'no you can't come to the White House', and Teddy Kennedy said, 'no, I'm not interested in meeting you', and the result of that was very shortly after that Gerry Adams makes this really significant statement about the IRA, and things really begin to move. I don't believe they would have begun to move if there had not been some very clear, not just statements, but actions by people who were important to them in the process that said—enough, no more of that. And they knew it was real, and they knew it was serious and therefore they changed. And I think it has been like that all the way through. It's a combination of helping people to think about things and reflect on them and see new possibilities and alternative ways, and then closing off the old ways. It's not just a question of opening new doors. You've also got to close the old doors.

Things change quickly—it can happen with a few words, a statement, an unexpected initiative, and it sometimes happens when you least expect it. Just weeks after it offered to shoot the killers of Robert McCartney, the IRA was being taken in another direction—down the road towards the Paisley deal. Adams set the route in a speech in Belfast on 6 April 2005. This was no ordinary speech; it was an address to the IRA. He has spoken to that organisation many times in private in its Army Conventions and other meetings. This time, on this date, he was doing it publicly. It was the first signal that the armed struggle was coming to some formal end. In it, Adams posed a question to the IRA leadership:

Can you take courageous initiatives which will achieve your aims by purely political and democratic activity? I know full well that such historic decisions can only be taken in the aftermath of intense internal consultation. I ask that you [the leadership of Oglaigh na hEireann) initiate this as quickly as possible.

By July the IRA had answered in a statement read by one of its longest serving former prisoners, Seanna Walsh, a close friend of Bobby Sands. It was a statement of many headlines:

- There had been a formal order to end the armed campaign;
- This would take effect from four o'clock on the afternoon of July 28th 2005—the date of the statement;
- All IRA units had been ordered to dump arms;
- And, the IRA leadership authorised its representative (Brian Keenan) to engage with the Independent International Commission on Decommissioning (IICD) to complete the process of putting arms beyond use;
- Two independent Church witnesses (Harold Good and Alec Reid) would witness and testify to this.

The long war was over. Its end was signalled in that statement read by Seanna Walsh and confirmed in the decommissioning process, and then in the republican decision to support policing. The IRA was emerging from its war into the political process. Soon, one member of its Army Council would sit in government with the man who had vowed to smash Sinn Féin. There had been no sackcloth, no ashes, no surrender or photographs, no victory or defeat, but peace and politics had finally been given shape through once unthinkable compromises. The Paisley–Provo deal was beginning to happen, and this just weeks after that statement from the IRA offering to shoot the killers of Robert McCartney; it was mind-boggling in its speed. The republican hand was forced in the aftermath of the robbery and the McCartney killing because as a movement it had to restore credibility to itself and to the peace process. Then, once it happened, it closed down Paisley's choices; he had to say yes because 'no' was no longer an option. The republican initiatives ordered by the Army Council were fashioned and designed to create that very outcome.

Chapter 4

Guns—Seeing and hearing is believing

What I heard was every bit as important, every bit as important. Had I only seen but not heard, I wouldn't have been as confident. Because, as we all know, it is not impossible to re-equip an army very quickly. So, what we needed to know was the decommissioning of the intent to ever go there again.
(CHURCH WITNESS REV. HAROLD GOOD ON SEEING
AND HEARING THE IRA'S DECOMMISSIONING.)

That decommissioning was testament—testament—of their veracity, of their sincerity, of their genuine-ness. And Paisley seen that too ... If an IRA man gives up his gun, there's only politics left.
(FORMER UVF LEADER GUSTY SPENCE COMMENTING
ON THE SIGNIFICANCE OF THE IRA PUTTING ITS ARMS
BEYOND USE.)

I would suppose the hardest time for the individual members of the IRA were the weeks before the actual decommissioning event when the weapons were collected from individuals and from dumps, and then it was clear for everybody—this is it ... The decommissioning event (itself) was technical work.
(BRIGADIER TAUNO NIEMINEN OF THE INDEPENDENT
INTERNATIONAL COMMISSION ON DECOMMISSIONING.)

You could lose at the negotiating table what you had won on the battlefield if you didn't have good leadership and a disciplined Movement. And I think that's one of the reasons why the decommissioning process took so long. Because people had to be very cautious, they had to be mindful of the dead, the sacrifice and the suffering, and whilst you could never do justice to the dead and the suffering that had taken place, at the same time you had to do your best and show a result for it …

I think it was stretched out and stretched out and stretched out because the republican base had not reached the stage of assurance and comfort with the peace process.

(FORMER REPUBLICAN LEADER AND IRA MEMBER
DANNY MORRISON SPEAKING TO THE AUTHOR.)

I want you to think about something for a few minutes. Think about all of the planning and the secret contacts, all of the hoops through which the IRA had to jump, all the risks that had to be taken in order to amass a stockpile of weapons. Think about how the IRA smuggled Libyan arms into Ireland in the mid-1980s and kept them hidden until they were used in the war. Then, think about how they became the lynchpin of the peace. One can see the level of mental struggle that must have been involved in emptying those weapons bunkers in order to ensure peace, on however tentative terms. The two processes—stockpiling and emptying—were achieved in equally secretive ways, but the leap of faith required to put weapons beyond use is one of the extraordinary events of the peace process in Ireland.

In all this, I am not sure that Trimble and Paisley ever really understood the IRA, ever really appreciated the complexities of the arms issue, what it meant for republicans and just how difficult it was for them to argue for and to achieve decommissioning. Both men made the same mistake of making demands that were impossible to meet, for various pressing reasons. As a result, on the weapons issue, Trimble and Paisley never got what they asked for. While no one could expect or ask those unionist leaders to see the IRA as that organisation sees itself, it was incumbent upon them to try to see these situations from the IRA's point of view in order to try to understand the many motives and obstacles. If they were ever to grasp the seriousness of the arms issue, they would have to understand what exactly those weapons meant to the IRA. They meant the IRA could not be defeated. As far as the IRA was concerned, those weapons had been made necessary by the very people—British and unionist—who were now asking for them to be handed over.

Accordingly, this was never going to be surrender, but when and how it was done was hugely significant. The truth of the matter was that the republican war was decommissioned along with those weapons. It meant that the armed struggle was over, and that fact had been accepted inside and across the mainstream IRA organisation. That, of course, required them to have a lot of faith and trust in their one-time enemies. There was a history to the arms issue that non-republicans might well have preferred to forget. Those weapons had only come into play after 1969, the streets and houses of Belfast were burning and republicans were unable to defend their community. It is a time Danny Morrison, who was a teenager then, remembers well:

> That experience of not having weapons, and people being burned out … and seeing people with wee bits of sticks of furniture on the back of lorries, and becoming refugees, and people saying, 'Where the fuck is the IRA?' … So, for my generation, August '69 meant that there was a responsibility

on republicans never to leave the nationalist community defenceless.

He will also tell you that 'the armed struggle did not appear out of thin air', that 'it was fifty years in the making' and that August 1969 was a big part of that. Morrison, a one-time republican leader and member of the IRA, can talk you through the importance of those Libyan weapons and why decommissioning 'looked like an ambush—a political ambush':

> It had never been raised in the Republican Movement as a realistic and necessary development in the process. And, okay, I know you finesse certain things and [consider] the implications and repercussions down the road. For example, I knew that when it came to [political] compromise the compromise was going to be a Northern Assembly ... but August '69 and the experience made the weapons issue much more complex—more complex for our generation than, for example, de Valera's generation.

Morrison remembers the IRA of the 1970s, a time when it was 'really poorly armed' and 'its supply line, even in terms of homemade explosive, appeared to be very, very low'. He knows how the Libyan weapons changed all of that. Of course, British Intelligence would have known that the IRA was looking for new supply routes in order to, as Morrison describes it, 'bring in proper weapons, more modern weapons, more effective weapons, which could alter the balance of the military struggle':

> 'They [British Intelligence] would have been aware of that. They spent a lot of resources trying to prevent that, trying to penetrate, but they obviously never were able to penetrate the IRA at a senior level. And proof of that [was] the mortar attack on Downing Street [in 1991], the Brighton bomb [in

1984], and the fact that [from] August '85 onwards that the
IRA had managed to bring in large [arms] shipments. And, of
course, I think that in retrospect you can see the professionalism of the IRA in that they weren't suddenly excited over
having these weapons. They actually stored these weapons,
put them away as they slowly built up ... in preparation for
an intensification in the tempo of the armed struggle.

By the time the *Eksund* was captured and the Libyan arms link
exposed in November 1987, it was too late. A huge supply of
guns and Semtex explosive had already got in under the radar
of the intelligence services, provoking a panic and a huge
search; little was found. On the other side of the coin was the
realisation within the republican organisation that the IRA 'was
armed to the teeth', and the next question was how to distribute
and use the new weapons.

'You had an expectation certainly that there was going to be
a dramatic shift in the war,' Morrison told me, although he had
long grown out of his own 'romantic and fantasy stage, and
[that] thought of driving the British Army into the sea'. The real
significance of the Libyan arms was that the IRA now 'had
enough *materiel* probably to last them, let's say, twenty years',
which in its eyes meant it 'couldn't be defeated'.

For all that, Morrison still knew that this was going to be a
very long war:

I think that the IRA is ideally suited to working on small-scale
operations, and not on large-scale operations. Obviously one
of the things [the IRA leadership] had to determine was, we
could, so to speak, flood the market with these weapons.
But, okay, you might have a massive amount of activity for a
year or two, but you'll also have a large number of fatalities,
casualties, losses, people going to jail in large numbers.
And that would be okay a gamble if the increase in tempo in

military operations brought about a sea change in political thinking in Britain. In other words [people saying], 'Look you [the Government] told us in 1977 that you were squeezing the IRA like a tube of toothpaste. You told us that the hunger strike was the IRA's last card. You told us this. You told us that, and, now, they're bombing England. Now, they're doing this.' And if that had come about [the sea change in thinking], then the strategy would have been the right strategy. But the IRA appears to have acted much more cautiously, and it found a level [of activity] and the weapons which suited its war best, and it turned out to be Semtex ... certainly Semtex turned out to be the most lethal of the IRA's weapons.

Morrison once described this period of the late 1980s as 'the Semtex War', but by 1991–92, when he was serving time in jail, even he was thinking in terms of ceasefire and negotiations. By that time the British had publicly acknowledged that the war was deadlocked in a stalemate. What Morrison could not contemplate, however, was decommissioning and he fully understands why the process of putting arms beyond use was so protracted and why it had to be done at the IRA's pace:

In the debates that we were having in jail, people were asking different questions, and there was a slogan that I remember somebody said once years ago, [that] you can't win at the negotiating table what you haven't won on the battlefield. But, I also added to it in a piece that I subsequently wrote— but you could lose at the negotiating table what you had won on the battlefield if you didn't have good leadership and a disciplined movement. And, I think, that's one of the reasons why the decommissioning process took so long, because people had to be very cautious, they had to be mindful of the dead, the sacrifice and the suffering that had taken place, and whilst you could never do justice to the dead and the suffering

that had taken place, at the same time you had to do your best
and show a result for it ... I think it was stretched out, and
stretched out, and stretched out because the republican base
had not reached the stage of assurance and comfort with the
peace process.

Morrison came to his own understanding of matters: 'In my head
I could live without the IRA's weapons provided I knew it was
replaced by a police service which was of us—trusted and representative of us—and that way that meant there could never
[again] be an August '69. Because my criteria [on the question
of the IRA's weapons] was could there be another August '69. If
there could be another August '69, the weapons had to be there.'

The leadership representative that the IRA eventually sent to
speak to the Independent International Commission on
Decommissioning (IICD) was Brian Keenan, a man identified
with rebuilding the republican organisation out of the turbu-
lence and turmoil of that period—1969 and soon afterwards.
Like Morrison, Keenan must have remembered that cutting
question back then: 'Where the fuck is the IRA?' He would have
felt at first-hand the hopelessness of that situation, how inade-
quate the IRA was, taunted by its own people with a new
acronym: I Ran Away. Like Morrison, too, he would have known
how the IRA struggled at times to sustain its war in the 1970s and
how the Libyan weapons changed everything. Unlike Morrison,
Keenan, along with others on the Army Council, would have to
make the decision on decommissioning. Given that background, it is not hard to see just how long a journey it was from
the humiliation of 1969 to Keenan's first meeting with the IICD
some thirty years later. It is also not hard to see why the subsequent process that was put in motion took so long to come to
fruition, more than five years later.

Andrew Sens, a member of the IICD, told me of his doubts
about the possibility of success in an interview for this book. He

spoke to me along with his Commission colleagues, Brigadier
Tauno Nieminen and General John de Chastelain, but none of
the three ever mentioned Brian Keenan's name to me.
Nonetheless, I know that he was the senior IRA representative
from the beginning to the end of the decommissioning process.
Sens describes that long process as follows:

> I don't know if anybody knows how many meetings we had
> with the IRA. There were quite a number. It wasn't just three
> or four in the course of that five years, and certainly in the first
> early meetings they were sceptical, I think. You know, we came
> from a different world, and what could we have in common
> —what kind of a basis could we have to communicate?
>
> They felt that they had concerns that had to be communi-
> cated, and they needed answers to questions, which only we
> could provide. I think there was perhaps some suspicion—
> perhaps it was on both sides, whether or not that communi-
> cation would work, but over the course of a number of
> meetings—quite a number of meetings in fact—we got to,
> [and] this is I think what you have been getting at when you
> talk about what is the psychological shift that took place over
> the five years, I think we came to an increasingly nuanced
> understanding of each other's requirements and capacities. I
> think in reflection that I was pleased that the three of us were
> able to deal with this situation in a way that was constructive,
> that led us to the point where it led to [in] 2005 [September
> 2005 and the major acts of IRA decommissioning] ... That, I
> don't think, was necessarily going to happen in 1999. It could
> well have broken down. It was by no means certain that we
> would be able to work out a framework of trust in which we
> could solve practical problems, that includes a methodology
> [for putting weapons beyond use]. That was certainly the
> most important practical problem.

September 2005 was the time of the real business of decommissioning. There had been three previous and much smaller 'events', during Trimble's time. Nieminen attaches significance to the first act in October 2001 because, however small or big, the IRA had 'stepped over that line' for the first time, a step that cemented its commitment to the process. That is the way Sens saw it: 'I think we had suspected if we could ever get a first decommissioning, it would then become a process and that process would inevitably lead to a conclusion ... but, getting that first step was hard.'

From their earliest conversations with republicans—with Martin McGuinness before Brian Keenan—the commissioners knew that all of this was going to take time, and that progress on the arms issue would depend on what else was happening in the political and security arenas:

> I don't think it's any secret [and] this did not come from our conversations with the IRA [representative] per se, but certainly our conversations with what I would call Professor McGuinness and our introduction to Irish politics ... For them [republicans] there was a structure here that was being built, and what they couldn't build was a house with a wall on one side, and have a roof that would stay up. If the roof were decommissioning, you had to have walls on both sides on which to rest the roof. So, that meant, yes, you've got to work through the decommissioning process—the modalities and the methods, but you've also got to do things about the problems that we've got ... with the administration of justice, the policing requirement and the profile of the military and all of the other elements in the political package. And you can't wrap and tie the bow on the package until everything is in the package.

So, that reality was understood from the very start of their contact with republicans. There were many moments of doubt at various stages, but Sens, Nieminen and de Chastelain are patient men, not given to excitement, and they knew this was going to be a marathon, not a sprint. They accepted that and therefore let it build incrementally from that first event in October 2001, as General de Chastelain describes:

> Well, we said at the time this is a significant event. We indicated that it was significant simply because … the mantra had always been, 'not one bullet—not one ounce'. And whilst the numbers, the amount of arms we dealt with in that event, we also mentioned was not huge, it was more than one bullet and more than one ounce. The fact that it had happened was important. And the second event was greater, and the third event was greater, but we wouldn't make it out to be greater than we felt it deserved to be. We were telling it like it was within the limitations that we could in terms of not saying exactly what it was, and that was one of the difficulties in 2003 [after the third decommissioning event] when I think some people (including David Trimble) would have liked us to have been a bit more expansive about what had happened, and we weren't.

They could not be more forthcoming because they had an understanding of confidentiality with the IRA representatives, which had been agreed in an almost lawyer-like fashion. Sens admits this was the case:

> They were very professional, and it's funny to use that word in this context. And good negotiators. They knew the negotiating process. You focus on an objective, and you prepare your fallbacks in advance. You don't wait until you didn't get what you wanted and decide what you're going to do next. They handled this in, you know, the best possible way.

They handled it their way, but it was too slow for Trimble. It was not about delaying tactics, but rather that the pace had to be carefully managed in tandem with the internal dynamics of the IRA. It simply could not be rushed, a fact Danny Morrison can understand in a way that unionists cannot or will not: 'We would have been in a worse situation, because a significant rump of republicans could have been so disillusioned that they could have turned against the leadership—and would that be in the interests of the unionist people?'

I suggested to him that the unionists could not understand that internal IRA process in the same way that he would. He replies: 'Yes, that is because of [their] moral elitism. That we [the unionists] are right. That we were the aggrieved people.'

This, he argues, remains the unionist position, admitting no responsibility for creating the circumstances out of which the IRA launched an armed struggle:

> To this day, I mean I have spoken to loyalists, loyalists have a completely different view of the 14th and 15th of August '69 than I have. I was down the Lower Falls [Road] when the place was on fire, and they were coming down the streets. I was only fifteen or sixteen, and I came back home before any-body was killed, but it was terrifying and it was seen as an invasion, and it was, again to sloganise, out of the ashes of Bombay Street arose the Provisionals.

The commissioners of the IICD had to tread carefully through all of these layers of history, trying to establish and build some trust as they went along. I asked de Chastelain—wearing his military hat—to reflect on that IRA journey:

> I suspect it was a difficult one, but understand we started talking to representatives in the IRA in the Fall of 1999, and the first event wasn't until 2001, and it was shortly after 9/11—

[so] play that around ... My own feeling is that they had decided by 1994 that it was over in the sense of an armed conflict leading to their aims, and acceptance that their aims could probably just as well be gained by political means— probably better by political means than by military ones. But that a number of issues stood in the way ... But I think their mind was made up at that time and that everything that happened between that and 2005 was seeing how much their political party would be listened to, the kind of achievements it might get in terms of getting into an Executive, getting certain issues like policing and justice and so forth looked after, and I guess the slowness of the movement towards completion (of decommissioning) was part and parcel of that.

Now, some might say that they were using it tactically. I wouldn't say that. They might have been. I don't know. Part of it was learning to build up some kind of trust between them and us from the point of view, not of liking each other, it was not a question of that, but of accepting the fact that we trusted them to do what they said they would do, and they trusted us to do what we said. And you may recall that very difficult time after the 2003 event when we did that press conference and we hadn't had much sleep, and it was a difficult circumstance. And I was asked, since we wouldn't specify exactly what it was [that had been decommissioned] other than a rather broad statement to the fact that it had been light, medium and heavy ordnance, if the British Government asked me to spell out in detail what it was would I tell them. And my answer was, yes of course I would, but I would then have to resign, because the basis on which we had agreed to do that event with the IRA was that it would remain in confidence, as the other events did, although we would take inventories and those inventories would be made available to the Government when the whole process of decommissioning—

not just IRA but the loyalists as well—was over. And I think to some extent that helped to, although it wasn't the intention, it helped to build the trust that they [the IRA] recognised we would do what we said we would do, and they would do what they said they would do. So that when they said in July of 2005 'the armed conflict is over and we will put our arms beyond use', we believed that that was the case, indeed they told us just before they made that public announcement.

Two months later, when those weapons, including many tons of the Libyan supplies, were put beyond use, the Reverend Harold Good was there to witness it. He was there as one of two Church witnesses, along with Fr Alec Reid. These two men were chosen because they were trusted and perhaps also because they had tried to understand. Harold Good has spent his life putting himself in other people's circumstances, trying to see through their eyes, and the republicans saw and appreciated that ability, as a source confirmed:

It was felt he was someone of integrity, and would stand over anything he was involved in. And if he was convinced that he was seeing the real thing, then you could be sure that he would say so and would defend that position.

It is very easy to condemn, much harder to see the reasons behind actions one abhors. Harold Good took the latter view; he saw people where others saw monsters. He told me he thought it strange when David Ervine asked him afterwards if he had felt honoured to be there. Thinking more about that question, he realised that what Ervine was getting at was that it was an honour to be trusted to be there, amidst the secrets of decommissioning. What does he himself think about his role?

Some people wonder how this guy Good got himself involved in all of that, and why would he? That was just all part of a journey, and during that journey I had come to understand something of what was going on within their [republican] thinking and from where they were coming. I disagreed totally with the way they were going about it.

I suppose it goes back even to when I was a very, very, junior minister—what we call a probationer, in the late '50s when I was posted to Bessbrook, South Armagh, and what was happening there was the first time I was caused to think about the history of my island, because I was seeing and hearing and experiencing what I never would have known or understood around that [IRA] border campaign. Curfews— the night I saw the people of Newry sit down in Market Square protesting against the curfew and being flushed out of the Square by water cannon, and people saying, 'that will be the end of that—that will cool them' … and I was very young and very inexperienced, but something within me prompted me to say, 'that was like putting fuel on a fire, whatever this is about'. And I'm not sure I fully understood, but I think all of that was the beginning of an understanding in my mind that this story wasn't just quite as simple and as straightforward and not as one-sided.

Harold Good also had the experience of working and living in divided communities outside of Northern Ireland. He had been challenged by those experiences to try to understand situations more clearly, to get under the surface, to explore and learn for himself, to make his own mind up rather than reading and speaking from the accepted scripts. He brought this approach back to Northern Ireland with him, and this is what brought him into contact with republicans long before the ceasefires and the coming of the peace process:

Some things that I experienced in the America of the '60s, not only things that I saw and observed and experienced in terms of the race issue there—a whole story in itself, ministering to a black congregation at the time that Martin Luther King was assassinated. And other stories where I had to become personally involved in trying to get a black-white couple out of a dreadful situation … and that consciously and unconsciously when I returned to Ireland influenced my whole way of approaching things in a way that perhaps otherwise might have escaped me. And I'd like to think that there were two things that republicans would have known about me when I became involved in all of that. One is that I perhaps had an understanding of where they were coming from, and, second, was I did not approve of the way they were going about it, but I'd an understanding, which meant that I had moved beyond blanket condemnation … so, we could have an honest relationship with an understanding of where each was coming from and could see each other as people and not necessarily as monsters. So that was a very important part of this journey. And it is a very hard thing to explain to other people who either haven't come to that place, or have no wish to come to that place.

The IRA was not condemned into ending its war, was not condemned into putting its arms beyond use. It was persuaded of a different way. And those, such as Harold Good, who tried to understand the republican mind, even though they were totally opposed to the IRA's armed struggle, played an important part in the making of the peace:

Once people know that you understand where they are coming from … it's less important to them that you agree with them. It is the honesty, it's the integrity of your debate that interests them—not that you are saying, 'oh it's okay', when they know that you know it's not okay.

Harold Good thought a lot about this; there was more to it than just witnessing the weapons being put away. He thought about the significance of these acts, what those guns had meant to the IRA, how the leadership had worked out with de Chastelain the method of putting that vast arsenal beyond use and then, having done that, how they worked their argument down through their organisation:

> I knew how important they [the weapons] were, not only from the point of view of their campaign as they saw it—their armed struggle—but historically. And I knew how within the constitution of republicanism that that was one of the two unpardonable crimes—to surrender your weapon. And how do you help people to move beyond something that within the [IRA] constitution is unpardonable to find a way. And I take my hat off to all of those—General de Chastelain and the negotiators on the republican side—who were able to find a formula which was acceptable to both British and Irish Governments to define in statute decommissioning in a way that they could live with, which they could take to their membership and sell it. That was remarkable, and we sometimes forget just, and I think the general public doesn't understand just how incredible that was to be able to come to that place. And people think it is a simple, easy thing. As we know from the events within loyalism, it is not an easy, simple thing … So, all of that, I think, is to say that you can't begin to contribute to a process until you genuinely understand where people are coming from—not a pretence, but genuinely, and you've got this thing called empathy, which doesn't mean for a moment that you agree or you are condoning.

That IRA process, involving de Chastelain and seen by the Church witnesses, has had an impact on the thinking of the veteran loyalist Gusty Spence. You can hear it in his new vocabulary: he no longer presents the argument that the weapons should be left to rust, and he accepts that what the IRA did has laid down a challenge for others. Now in his seventies, Spence is a thinking man, one clearly motivated by cause. He was one of the first men sent to jail in the war, is a former leader of the Ulster Volunteer Force (UVF) and the man chosen to deliver the ceasefire statement of the Combined Loyalist Military Command in October 1994, and then to read the endgame statement of the UVF in May 2007. This is an indication of the credibility he has within his own community. From his position on the other side of the lines, Spence is prepared to acknowledge the significance of what the IRA did, and is able to see it for all it meant in terms of ending the republican fight and contributing to the developing peace. He doesn't mince words:

It was momentous.

I for one would never have dreamt it would have happened in total, because they didn't have a history [of decommissioning]—[weapons] bunkered, yes, dumped whatever that means, yes, but they never had a history of decommissioning, and that decommissioning was testament—testament—of their veracity, of their sincerity, of their genuineness. And Paisley seen that too, and that's why they insisted on the arms, because if an IRA man gives up his gun, there's only politics left.

Spence knew enough to realise that, in whatever way the IRA would eventually deal with its weapons, it would be done in a way acceptable to the organisation, not in any way demanded and specified by others. However, he believes that in the way it was done it was done convincingly, in a way that not just Paisley but others had to accept. Most importantly, the method of decommissioning was credible enough to allow the political process to begin to move forward again, and it gained that credibility because of the word of the Church witnesses who accompanied the IRA and the de Chastelain team throughout this process:

> And I think it had, I can't only say on Paisley, I have to include in anything that Paisley done, I have to include Robinson ... he was as close as any confidant could possibly be ... So it was momentous, and I believe that was one of the turning points where Ian Paisley and the DUP said, 'right now, that's it' ... They [the IRA] are not armless [without guns]. They would have a couple of pikes in the thatch ... They could never ever have yielded to Paisley's demands for photographs and all the rest of it ... [So], they said ... we'll take a particular person or persons [with us as witnesses] who have standing in society, especially Alec Reid. Alec Reid was particularly close to the Provos, didn't agree with their tactics or whatever, but was a very, very, close confidant of Adams. Whenever I was speaking to Alec, I knew I was speaking directly to Gerry Adams.

Spence was convinced, as he believes others were, not just by the acts of decommissioning but by the later republican decision to support policing:

> I do believe, oh I do absolutely believe it, no question about it. And not only that, more than Gusty Spence believes it, the DUP believe it. Alongside decommissioning, I would say support for the police was extraordinary—extraordinary—but, then again, inevitable. They couldn't stay out of it.

Spence has the confidence to think and speak his mind. He says things that would not be popular in the loyalist and unionist communities, gives an analysis of the war and political failings that would make others uncomfortable, make them think about things they would much rather forget. He can do this because he is willing and capable of seeing things from a different perspective. Spence can read the IRA in a way that Trimble and Paisley could not, therefore he sees and says things in a way that the political leaders of unionism do not:

At one particular time, and I'm saying this as a loyalist, at one particular time there was no alternative to violence. Violence had to be committed on the republican side. There was no alternative because nobody was listening—nobody wanted to hear anything about all-Ireland or Sinn Féin or anything to do with nationalism. So, therefore, the violence that followed was inevitable.

This is Spence striving to understand in a way that others cannot and will not. The political and peace processes that brought everyone and everything to the negotiating table are what made a difference, they are what changed minds and ended the war, making possible the acts of decommissioning that for so long had been dismissed in the language of 'not a bullet, not an ounce'. As he thinks and speaks today, Spence believes that war could have been avoided if people had only been prepared to recognise the legitimacy of the political aspirations of others, and been able to consider the type of negotiated settlement we now have. So, with the great benefit of hindsight, what is Spence's last thought on the war:

Unnecessary—completely and absolutely unnecessary. If those people who had been involved in the war had had the political nous then, which they have now, it would have rendered that war unnecessary. Because whenever all is said and done—leave the republicans to one side—all the nationalists wanted was recognition, a piece of the cake, human rights.

In the end, decommissioning became as inevitable as arming had once been. The IRA undertook to commit to putting its weapons beyond use, what remained was to convince others of the level of that commitment. It was necessary for all involved to hear their promise, even they could not see the evidence with their own eyes. To that end, Harold Good and Alec Reid told a convincing and a compelling story of what they had witnessed and were able to persuade the doubters, albeit some more quickly than others. Time has borne testament to that commitment, too—all the days since September 2005 in which not a bullet or a bomb has been heard. The IRA meant what it said when it pledged to end its armed campaign and it did move soon thereafter to dispose of its weapons. In the silence of its guns we can hear, as Spence put it, the genuineness of the words and actions that followed.

Harold Good heard it for himself in the company of republicans, heard it in those days he spent with Alec Reid, the IRA and General de Chastelain in September 2005. He has never discussed the procedures or the detail of what happened. I have advised him he should write it down, his thinking and his experience, so that it can be read many years from now as a contribution to the recording and the understanding of that period. For now, he speaks in more general terms, but when you listen you can see the picture and you can hear the message:

> People sometimes say, there is all this idea, had you a black bag over your head or whatever, and was it not very scary and all of that. I found myself, interestingly enough … for a lot of that week, I found myself in my pastoral mode. And by that I mean I was with people who were going through a whole process of change in their lives, and in that to which they had given the best years of their lives. What I heard was every bit as important, every bit as important. Had I seen but not heard, I wouldn't have been as confident, because as we all

know it's not impossible to re-equip an army very quickly. And so what we needed to know was the decommissioning of the intent to ever go there again. And so you had people who had given the best years of their lives to something that now had changed dramatically, and clearly had not achieved what they had either hoped or expected, or perhaps had been led to believe they would achieve ... I found myself having the kind of conversation with people—natural conversation with people who were re-thinking, re-thinking, where they were, and where they were going, and reflecting on where they had been, and to me that was actually, there were times when I found that moving to be entrusted not only with the task of seeing but ... just sitting while people were, in a very genuine way, just reflecting, and more importantly talking about where do we go from here ... and, again, to have people to trust you enough just to be reflecting.

These were not conversations of the hand-wringing type, not the stuff of 'we have done terrible things'. It was more a looking forward, seeing beyond these days in September 2005 and looking for the 'what next'. In one sentence Harold Good summarises what he believes he heard in those conversations: 'We have to find a new way, and a way that can embrace all the people of this island.'

Harold Good believed, was convinced, that the IRA 'wasn't going back'. In its reports, the IICD records the facts, but does not offer an interpretation or meaning. However, there was enough in its nine-paragraph report for the rest of us to be able to read between the lines. I have said before—and I have said it to General de Chastelain—that I do not believe the IRA would leave itself without guns. I accept Spence's assertion that there will always be a pike in the thatch and I believe that is due to the humiliating experience of 1969. On the other hand, I also accept Harold Good's description that in this period the intent was decommissioned, the war was ended and that there is no going back. Furthermore, I believe all of that was confirmed, in the later republican initiative on policing.

REPORT OF THE INDEPENDENT INTERNATIONAL COMMISSION ON DECOMMISSIONING, SEPTEMBER 26, 2005

1 Over the past number of weeks we have engaged with the IRA representative in the execution of our mandate to decommission paramilitary arms.

2 We can now report that we have observed and verified events to put beyond use very large quantities of arms which the representative has informed us includes all the arms in the IRA's possession. We have made an inventory of this *materiel*.

3 In 2004 the Commission was provided with estimates of the number and quantity of arms held by the IRA. These estimates were produced by the security forces in both jurisdictions and were in agreement. Our inventory is consistent with these estimates and we believe that the arms decommissioned represent the totality of the IRA's arsenal.

4 The manner in which the arms were decommissioned is in accordance with the remit given us by the two governments as reflected in their Decommissioning Acts of 1997.

5 A Protestant and a Catholic clergyman also witnessed all these recent events: the Reverend Harold Good, former President of the Methodist Church in Ireland, and Father Alec Reid, a Redemptorist priest.

6 The new single inventory of decommissioned IRA arms incorporates the three we made during the preceding IRA events. This lists all the IRA arms we have verified as having been put beyond use. We will retain possession of this inventory until our mandate is complete.

7 We can report, however, that the arms involved in the recent events include a full range of ammunition, rifles, machine guns, mortars, missiles, handguns, explosives, explosive substances and other arms, including all the categories described in the estimates provided by the security forces.

8 In summary, we have determined that the IRA has met its commitments to put all its arms beyond use in a manner called for by legislation.

9 It remains for us to address the arms of the loyalist paramilitary groups, as well as other paramilitary organisations, when these are prepared to co-operate with us in doing so.

Tauno Nieminen, John de Chastelain, Andrew Sens, 26 September 2005

Of course, the rest of us will continue to wonder what it was like to have been there—amongst all of those guns and bullets. What was it like to be part of an historic process that was ending a war? When you ask the men who signed that report for their thoughts, they will tell you there was little time for thinking. As Andrew Sens says:

It was a technical week for us. It was not a week of reflection, or stock-taking or an emotional week of catharsis. For us it was getting up before six, getting to bed after midnight, and, in between, you were working your head off, trying to get a sandwich so that you survived the experience, and that was certainly true of the team of interlocutors [from the IRA] with whom we were working—all of us in the same boat. It was a nuts and bolts week … any emotional catharsis came afterwards … I had a huge sense of relief that this had come to something … we had actually got something really worthwhile done, and it gave me an immense sense of pleasure, but I didn't feel that that week when I was doing it. It was only after the press conference.

That was when Tauno Nieminen also sensed the importance of what had been achieved: 'When we got to the Culloden Hotel, into that hall, we saw all the TV cameras and the flashes going off. That was the moment for me when I realised we had done something significant.'

The Finnish brigadier also added this thought:

I suppose the hardest time for the individual members of the IRA were the weeks before the actual decommissioning event when the weapons were collected from individuals and from dumps, and then it was clear for everybody—this is it … The decommissioning event [itself] was technical work.

You get an idea of that technical side to all of this in the words of General John de Chastelain—the counting and the weighing, the mental calculations at each location, understood to be nine and spread across 'quite a lot of territory', the writing of inventories and ensuring that everything tallied with the estimates provided by the security forces, North and South:

Some of the items we dealt with were ammunition in their original boxes from the (Libyan arms) shipments that hadn't been opened. We opened them to count. We also had sacks of ammunition which we had to sort to get different calibres. So, we would weigh a certain number of calibres and then put all those calibres in a sack and weigh that so that we would get a calculation of the number. And the fact that they were in sacks and mixed seemed clear to us that people had gone from dump, to dump, to dump to gather stuff up. Now, ask me to prove that and I can't, but it certainly made sense that

that was in the distributive system that they had, that was the kind of thing you would expect to see happen … It was a very busy week … but the intent was clear on the part of the people with whom we were dealing. It was clear to us from what they told us, and from what we saw and what we did, a lot of work had gone into gathering this stuff in such a way that led us to believe that, yes, it was what they said—everything. They made the point there may be a few things that were missing because people died, and they work on a distributive system, but, to the best of their knowledge, this was everything, and we accepted that … So, it was a tough week, we were extremely busy. It was difficult for them too, I think. Some of their volunteers probably weren't particularly happy that they were having to do it, but they were doing it … [because] that is the determination of the leadership, and that's what we're going to do.

And that is why it was done—because the Army Council ordered it done. The three commissioners were, I think, able to detach themselves from the emotion and wider meaning of that week. They were not part of our war, they were outsiders brought in to do a job, which they did. For the IRA, on the other hand, it was a very different kind of week, as an anonymous republican source confirmed during an interview for this book:

I think that for the bulk of the Army [the IRA] it was for them, I think, a massive psychological challenge. It just struck such a raw nerve at all levels in the Army from the ground upwards … that was an extremely difficult period for people.

But I have to say that by that stage the work that was done by the leadership preparing people for it [had helped] … I know nobody who supported it, but few if any were prepared to do anything about it at that stage, because you were talking eleven years down the line [since the original ceasefire of 1994], a long period of managing people's moods and emotions, and also I think the benefits—the political benefits—that were out there, Sinn Féin replacing the SDLP as the majority party in the North, the prisoners out of prison, there were a lot of things that people could see were beneficial, the police changing—all of that sort of stuff. And I just think that republicans who were of a mindset to oppose it would have opposed inside their own heads. In other words you couldn't have taken a straw poll [inside the IRA] on whether they should do it or not, because it would never have happened. So, in my opinion, this was leadership at its best.

That leadership would be needed again. Before the deal with Paisley, before the making of the new government, there was more to be done and arguably what was to come was bigger than ceasefire, bigger than ending the armed campaign, bigger than decommissioning. The next question was one that had proved a fatal stumbling block in the past: the issue of policing.

Chapter 5

Policing—The bitter pill

I remember around the time of the name change around policing, if Ronnie Flanagan [had] said, 'I want you to walk up the street in the nude', people would have walked up the street in the nude ... I'm not sure Hugh Orde could have delivered that bit of it. So it's the same in terms of Sinn Féin leadership. You needed the McGuinness', the Adams', the public figures, the people who had to deliver that change. And it was almost—if we want you to walk up the street in the nude, they would have walked up the street in the nude.
(ASSISTANT CHIEF CONSTABLE PETER SHERIDAN COMMENTING ON THE IMPORTANCE OF LEADERSHIP FIGURES IN CHANGING ATTITUDES ON POLICING.)

In my time probably the most significant event in terms of the strategic development of Northern Ireland and indeed policing.
(CHIEF CONSTABLE SIR HUGH ORDE, SPEAKING IN SEPTEMBER 2007, ON THE REPUBLICAN ENDORSEMENT OF POLICING EARLIER THAT YEAR.)

I must say there was even people in our party saying we will not get them (republicans) that far. Don't raise it. It will become another decommissioning millstone around our necks. But it didn't ... that was

the *objective that had to be achieved, the policing
one ... Getting them to accept the legitimacy of that
Crown Force was far more important ideologically
and practically than any other issue.*
(IAN PAISLEY JUNIOR COMMENTING ON HOW
REPUBLICAN SUPPORT FOR POLICING BECAME
THE POLITICAL DEALMAKER IN 2007.)

*They [the police] certainly were the frontline—some
people say storm troopers—they certainly were the
frontline, and the front military line in the State
fighting against republicanism ... They had to be
changed ... My history has been the IRA, and clearly
during that period, I mean I was very proud of it, but
clearly you're in a fighting mode. When you enter
politics, when you enter negotiations, you've to
remove yourself certainly from the fighting mode,
but certainly that doesn't mean to say that all of a
sudden you're compromising on everything. You're
still in a battle to try to get equality, to try to get a
proper police service, etc. etc.*
(SINN FÉIN JUNIOR MINISTER GERRY KELLY ON HIS
JOURNEY FROM WAR TO POLITICS.)

Stormont, 13 December 2006: every picture tells a story, and this one spoke very loudly about one of the most significant developments in the peace process. Hugh Orde, in his police uniform, sat at one side of the table and Gerry Adams at the other side. They had first met a couple of years earlier in Downing Street, but this meeting was different. This was for everyone to see, an image that was intended to speak to republicans and to tell the story of the next steps that would be taken. An enemy relationship was ending.

It was conditioning people, normalising a bit of this … and that's what they were doing—conditioning their own people, even in their own thoughts and minds [saying], 'we're on the move here, we're on the run down the hill here on this folks'. It sort of galvanised that thinking.

Such are the thoughts of the Assistant Chief Constable Peter Sheridan, who was also in the room that day. These meetings do not just happen, they are thought about and talked about before the door opens and we are allowed to see inside. At Stormont's Parliament Buildings at 9.30am on the morning of Wednesday, 13 December 2006, we watched the ground being prepared for arguably the most significant republican initiative of the peace process. This was not just a meeting between Orde and Adams, it was a watershed moment in the transition from all that happened in the past, into a new future where the police and republicans would no longer be enemies.

Orde described to me those early engagements, the first discussions after those bloody years of stand-off:

One thing that I've learned since we started to engage is the lack of knowledge within Sinn Féin on policing. Now, should we be surprised? Not really. If you disengage with something for thirty-five years, if you actively had a propaganda campaign to rubbish anything that was constructive within policing, it's not surprising you don't know much about it. But I was a bit surprised because their machine generally is quite effective and efficient. I just think they didn't have the wit to work out what it is they would need to know … about the reality of policing. Now, in fairness, as it has developed, they clearly, if you look at the Policing Board, they are clearly engaged—a lot of note-taking and questions. Our engagement strategy was open house in the sense that if you want to learn, if you want to understand, we'll make whatever you need available, and I think that's started to work. But I do think the more they understand how complex policing is through the day-to-day engagement, the more they'll understand the key issues for their community are exactly the same [as elsewhere].

For many years the only thing republicans knew and understood was that the police force, the Royal Ulster Constabulary (RUC), was on the other side in the war. When republicans thought about the police, they thought about the Special Branch, the dirty war, the secret bugging and surveillance. When they thought about policing, it was about monitoring patrolling patterns, planning attacks, preparing counter-interrogation strategies; they never thought about the nuts-and-bolts of everyday police work.

Several times I asked the question of the former Chief Constable Sir Ronnie Flanagan and other senior officers: could the police force that fought the war against the IRA police the peace? The bottom line was that on the issue of policing Northern Ireland, it wasn't just the republicans who needed to change their thinking—police officers at every level in the organisation needed to tackle and change their prevalent attitudes and thinking, too. It demanded an overhaul on both sides. The police force underwent a process of sweeping reforms, as directed in the recommendations of the *Patten Report*. The first thing to change was the name: the RUC became the PSNI—the Police Service of Northern Ireland.

Sir Hugh Orde has been the Chief Constable of the PSNI since September 2002. In that photographed meeting with Adams on 13 December 2006, he insisted on wearing uniform. The Secretary of State Peter Hain had asked, on Adams' behalf, that he not wear uniform. Adams also spoke directly to Orde about this, which indicates how sensitive and how difficult the handling of this transition was. Orde tactfully describes those background discussions as follows:

A number of people were keen for me not to turn up in uniform. I would not have turned up in anything else. I'm a cop. They wanted to meet the cops, not anyone else, and cops wear uniform. But also I was going to [the] Police Board afterwards, and I made the absolute point, I would meet them [Sinn Féin] early, because I was not being late for that [other] meeting. The point was I'd be at [the] Police Board at eleven o'clock that morning, because that's when I'm always at Police Board … because it's that important.

(The Policing Board is a committee of politicians and independent members who are tasked with holding the PSNI to account. It emerged out of the Patten reforms, but Sinn Féin, as part of its police boycott, refused to take its seats on the Board. Later, a policy shift and a new direction would see Sinn Féin occupy those seats and become fully involved in the policing structures.)

One cannot underestimate the significance of that meeting, that moment in the process. I wrote at the time that Adams would not have gone into that room to be photographed with Orde if he did not intend going further and taking others with him. This, as Peter Sheridan has described it, was all part of the preparation for the march towards a new policing and political arrangement. When you put together the policing initiative, the acts of decommissioning and the formal ending of the IRA's armed campaign, you see the new context in which the deal with Paisley and the DUP was achieved. This was not a token republican endorsement of policing. It meant so much more than that. You can end a ceasefire; we had seen that happen in 1996 in the bombing of London. You can replace weapons that have been decommissioned; the IRA has the engineering capability to do that. However, you cannot encourage young people from your community to join the police one day and then shoot at them the next. It represents a whole new departure, a truly radical shift in policy and attitude, and therein lay the monumental significance of republicans' agreement to join the policing system. Orde needs only one sentence to explain its worth:

> In my time, probably the most significant event in terms of the strategic development of Northern Ireland, and indeed policing.

Orde was able to look at all that was happening in a way that was not coloured or distorted by what had gone before. He had not been part of the war, had not been in Northern Ireland for all those years of killing. He had knowledge of the violence and of the nature of the war through his work with the Stevens Investigation, which examined the murder of solicitor Pat Finucane and the wider question of security forces collusion, but he had not served on the frontline. So he understood that there was more than one side in all this, that there were in fact many sides to the Northern Ireland story.

Gerry Kelly agrees that Orde's distance from the day-to-day realities of the war on the streets made it easier for republicans to deal with him:

> He was not weighed down with having to fight the war, which for instance Ronnie Flanagan did, also with the baggage that comes with it.
>
> You have to remember this, and I am not saying this in any way of saying that it was all one-sided, but there was a shoot-to-kill policy, there was internment, there was literally tens of thousands of house raids, there were people killed with plastic bullets, interrogation, all of that. I'm not saying that to give a list of what they did, but when you then are looking at someone across the table who maybe was entirely involved in that … then it clearly is harder to try and deal with those circumstances. To answer your question, yes, it's easier in terms of the atmosphere involved.

Orde had the benefit of a clean sheet. However, he has shown himself capable, at times, of speaking with all the tact and subtlety of a sledgehammer. He even offered—mischievously, I suspect—to address Sinn Féin's Special Árd Fheis on policing. What's more, he stated this publicly, at a time when republicans were grappling with this most difficult and delicate of issues. Yet, he got away with it, and in a way that Sir Ronnie Flanagan would not have. Gerry Kelly is circumspect in his reading of that unprecedented offer:

> I do think that the public aspect of it became a problem. It didn't help, and I think we let him know that. But I don't know if he was doing it mischievously, and I don't see the reason for him to do it mischievously. Now, and it's an interesting thing, because maybe if it had of been Ronnie Flanagan, your immediate reaction would have been—he's mixing. Whereas at least I have some doubt with Hugh Orde. There clearly was some naïvety.

What Orde was offering was as daft as Martin McGuinness suggesting that he address the annual conference of the Police Federation. Nonetheless, this incredibly delicate process of police reform needed someone like Orde, someone who was detached from the emotional scars of the past. Orde could not have delivered the RUC in the way that Flanagan did, but he was better suited to achieve the aims of this new era and to prepare the ground inside policing for republican participation. 'It was difficult for my people too,' is an important point that Orde often reiterates. Gerry Kelly accepted that when I asked him if he understood that point:

> Did I understand it? Entirely. In a way that is one of the essential elements I think both of negotiations and of conflict resolution—that you are able, in your own way, because

clearly they cannot get into my mind, but … they had to make some effort to understand republicanism to be able to move away from where they were. We, of course, had to have some understanding [of their feelings]. In fact, republicans would not have thanked me at times for saying not all cops are bad.

When Orde and Adams met on 13 December 2006, there were some present in that room who had known at first-hand the cost of the war, including Peter Sheridan. I wrote at the time that I would give a thousand pennies and more for their private thoughts. Sheridan had known the war through his service in the RUC. He remembered well the dangers inherent in an officer's journey to and from work, the threat of booby-trap bombs and attacks on police vehicles, stations and personnel. Just over 300 police officers were killed and many more were wounded. For Sheridan, that process of reform leading to an inclusive police service must have brought difficulties, and difficult memories:

Whilst I understood the threat, and particularly when I was in Derry, I was under no illusions about what the threat was. And people [the IRA] had my details and targeted me where I went to church and targeted my family and home and all that sort of stuff. So I wasn't naïve around all of that, but nevertheless I didn't let it interfere with my day-to-day working and it didn't become all consuming, and I think that's probably how a lot of police officers probably managed that. Yes, it was in the back of your head, and, yes, it was there constantly … I'm not saying it wasn't in your mind, but it wasn't always at the forefront of my mind—[wasn't] everything that I thought and did. I wasn't stupid around measures that you took to protect yourself, but nor did I let it rule my life. It was one side that was shooting and killing police officers—murdering police officers.

Quiet player: Harold Good (*above*) helped in the making of the peace, and observed in the moment photographed below the real 'hand of history' confirming the deal between Ian Paisley and Martin McGuinness. (ᴍᴛ *Hurson/Harrison Photography*)

(*Reuters*)

The beginning of the new beginning. The St Andrews talks bring closer the government of Ian Paisley and Martin McGuinness. (*PA Photos/Topfoto*)

A new man in charge. After long years of waiting, Peter Robinson's leadership moment finally arrived. (*PA Photos/Topfoto*)

Danny Morrison, a long-time republican strategist: 'The head had to rule the heart, and the head knew we were in a military stalemate.' (*MT Hurson*)

The men who made it possible: Prime Ministers Tony Blair and Bertie Ahern answered the Irish question. (PA *Photos/Topfoto*)

A General's opinion. Army GOC Nick Parker avoids the word 'war'. It was a campaign, a fight, a challenge, a mission … (© *Crown Copyright/*MOD)

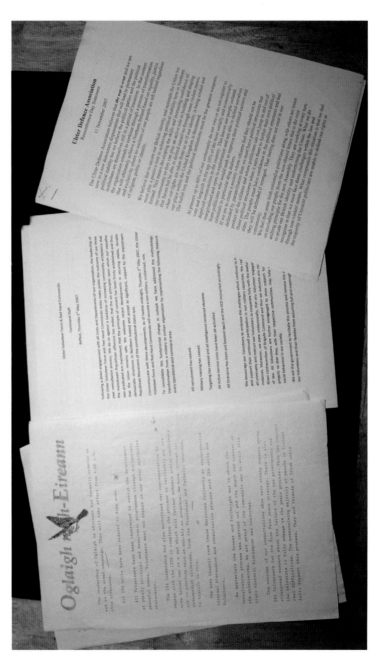

Their wars are over. The statements that changed the IRA, the UVF and the UDA. (MT *Hurson*)

Representatives of Óglaigh na hÉireann met with Brídgeen Hagans,
the partner of Robert McCartney, and with his sisters before
our statement of 25 February was issued.

The meeting lasted five and a half hours. During this time the
IRA representatives gave the McCartney family a detailed account
of our investigation.

Our investigation found that after the initial melee in Magennis's
bar a crowd spilled out onto the street and Robert McCartney,
Brendan Devine and two other men were pursued into Market Street.
.... were involved in the attacks in Market Street on the
evening of 30 January. A fifth person was at the scene. He
took no part in the attacks and was responsible for moving
to safety one of the two people accompanying Robert McCartney
and Brendan Devine.

- One man was responsible for providing the knife that was used
in the stabbing of Robert McCartney and Brendan Devine so

The IRA representatives detailed the outcome of the internal
disciplinary proceedings thus far and stated in clear terms
that the IRA was prepared to shoot the people directly involved
in the killing of Robert McCartney.

The McCartney family raised their concerns with the IRA
representatives.

These included:

Firstly, the family made it clear that they did not want physical
action taken against those individuals involved. They stated that they wanted
those individuals to give a full account of their actions in
court.

Secondly, they raised concerns about the intimidation of witnesses.

The IRA's position on this was set out in unambiguous and categoric
was on February 15 and February 25. Before and after this
ting with the family the IRA

Always capable of shocking. More than a decade after its ceasefire, the IRA offers to shoot those who killed Robert McCartney. (MT Hurson)

The author's Stormontgate notes. MI5 believe Rowan's reports resulted from a breach of the Official Secrets Act. (*MT Hurson*)

It's 'laughable'. PSNI Chief Constable Sir Hugh Orde dismissed republican claims that Stormontgate was a 'securocrat' plot. (PA *Photos/Topfoto*)

Learning about conflict. Students from the University of Pittsburgh in conversation with the author. (*Tony Novosel*)

A week in politics. All smiles from Denis Donaldson after the 'Stormontgate' case collapses in court. (PA *Photos/Topfoto*)

Seven days later, 'I was a British agent.' The confession that cost Donaldson his life. (PA *Photos/Topfoto*)

From behind the mask. The UVF spoke to the author as it prepared to leave its war stage.
(*John Nicholson*)

An ageing face. The veteran loyalist Gusty Spence with the words of the UVF's endgame.
(*Pacemaker Press International*)

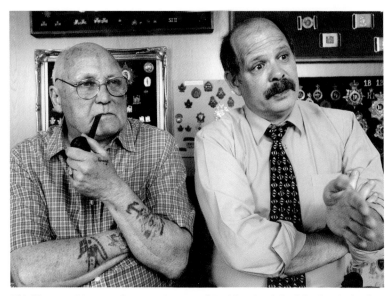

Thinking men. Mentor and protégé, Spence and David Ervine, helped develop the loyalist ceasefire and peace strategies. (MT *Hurson*)

The new face and voice of political loyalism. Dawn Purvis became leader of the Progressive Unionist Party after the sudden death of David Ervine. (MT *Hurson*)

The three men of decommissioning: Brigadier Tauno Nieminen, John de Chastelain and Andrew Sens, no doubt wiser for all their lectures on Irish history. (*Aaro Suonio*)

Their news conference in 2005, and the moment the arms penny really dropped. The IRA's guns had been taken out of Irish politics. (*Taina Suonio*)

Taken on a nervous journey. The republicans Jim Gibney (opposite) and Tom Hartley crossed the lines into the loyalist community to offer their condolences after David Ervine's death. (MT *Hurson*)

Witness — seeing and hearing is believing. The churchman Harold Good watched as the weapons were put beyond use. (*MT Hurson*)

The 'back channel'. Derryman Brendan Duddy was for years the secret link between the British and Martin McGuinness. (*Courtesy of the Duddy family*)

So, whilst there would have been a loyalist paramilitary threat, they weren't perceived to be attacking the State or police officers. So, naturally, the enemy relationship, as you call it, would have been with the IRA. And you're absolutely right, if you are going to move in any relationship with trust, then it has to be the building of those relationships, and those small bits of trust-building that happen at the very start of it, and people start to say, 'Well I think I can trust him', or 'I know that you can trust him', and then that starts to create a seed.

The problem was that for so long this had been a relationship of zero trust and zero respect. There was no room for compassion or understanding amidst the bullets and the blasts. Earlier, Gerry Kelly gave a flavour of how republicans viewed the old RUC: rubber and plastic bullets, live rounds, shoot-to-kill, house searches, harassment, humiliation, a police force that was identified with one side of the community and with taking that side's part in all situations. Each side, therefore, brought its own difficult memories into the room, which gives some perspective as to just how crucial and fragile this process was. One republican source described the policing initiative as follows:

There are two or three issues that compete with each other in terms of their emotional strain on republicans. The IRA itself calling a ceasefire, putting their weapons beyond use, calling the armed struggle off and, then, this whole question of what to do with the police—and endorsing the police … The IRA killed them, they killed the IRA, people were brutalised, so, the emotional aspect of this, I think, the psychological aspect of it was very, very, difficult for republicans. And to this day, even still, republicans grapple with this whole notion of engaging with the PSNI. Because people just feel that they are part of the enemy, and, so, therefore they are seen as that, and we have a bit to travel in relation to getting into the heads of nationalists and republicans that the PSNI should be supported and that they are a police service ... What you have to remember in all of this is so much of it was unthinkable just a short period of time ago. Ten years ago it was unthinkable that republicans would be putting their arms beyond use, that they would be considering calling the armed struggle off, and not only that, but actually endorsing the Police Service of Northern Ireland. And for a lot of people it's theological, is probably the best way of describing it. These are points of theology—republican theology—that challenge your psyche, the framework in which you have lived your entire life either inside the IRA, inside Sinn Féin or whatever the case might be. So, I just think that it is touchstone stuff, it's raw stuff ... [and] that the leadership were prepared to lead in that direction says a lot about them.

Like the Paisley–McGuinness relationship, the police–republican relationship was something that challenged everyone's thinking. That these one-time enemies came to form an essential part of the peace is a testament to strong leadership on both sides. Republicans present Ronnie Flanagan as one of the bogeymen of the war; on the police side, Martin McGuinness is viewed in the same way. However, it was the credentials and the standing of Flanagan inside the RUC and McGuinness inside the Republican movement that made much of the change possible. Their willingness to consider and work towards an alternative opened the minds of others. I asked Peter Sheridan how he viewed the republican leadership's management of its movement in the debate on policing:

> Probably others could learn from it. Some of it is about how disciplined an organisation it was, which allowed it probably that sort of iron fist approach to things, which made people

follow it … I think they were probably, during what I call that Cold War period when there was still a stand-off between Sinn Féin and the police, and there still is a bit of that Cold War although it's continually warming, but during that time they were able to manage their own people sufficiently well to bring them through, not that it was without dissention. Once you're in a disciplined organisation, you'll do what you're told on this, and the grouping did.

They used, of course they used, the whole of the organisation. But there are also, like it or not, charismatic people in it. There are people who, as individuals, people would follow, and they had an image about them that people liked. Without putting it into the same context, but I remember around the time of the name change around policing, if Ronnie Flanagan [had] said, 'I want you to walk up the street in the nude', people would have walked up the street in the nude … I'm not sure Hugh Orde could have delivered that bit of it. So it's the same in terms of Sinn Féin leadership. You needed the McGuinness', the Adams', the public figures, the people who had to deliver that change. And it was almost—if we want you to walk up the street in the nude, they would have walked up the street in the nude.

Sheridan is putting it in simple, easy-to-understand terms, but his analysis is sound. Key individuals in different leadership positions made important arguments in different phases of this process that allowed things to progress to the next stage. Had they thought differently, argued differently, they would have been heard and followed along another route. That was the influence and the contribution of people such as Flanagan and McGuinness.

Adams and Orde had first begun discussions on the policing issue in November 2004, in Downing Street. Tony Blair and his officials were in the room that day. Orde was not in uniform and there was no photographer to capture the scene. This was a tentative beginning and the republican agenda for the meeting was demilitarisation—a discussion on the mechanics of how and when the British Army would vacate its posts and stations in Northern Ireland. Orde was there to talk about policing, of course, but the republicans were not yet ready for the type of initiative they would take in the early part of 2007. What interests me about this meeting—and with the others on this issue— are the private thoughts of those involved. When I spoke with Peter Sheridan about the policing question, I wanted to get beyond the routine text of what the republicans said and what the police said. I asked him what it was really like being in a room with the enemy. What was he thinking? Were they what he expected them to be, or were they something different?

> I'll tell you honestly what came into my head. And it wasn't to do with my own difficulties [or those] my family had— having to move out of our house at one stage and all the security work around the house. And it wasn't all the day-to-day hassles that you had.

He told me a personal story about a very close friend of his 'whose father was murdered' by the IRA. 'He was in nothing,' Sheridan said. 'He was mistaken as a police officer.' Many years later, Sheridan's friend told him she had voted for the Good Friday Agreement because she wanted a 'better life for her kids'. 'But,' he went on, 'she couldn't forgive one person—and that was Martin McGuinness. Right, wrong or indifferent, in her mind that was the face—*that* was the face.'

So this is what was in Sheridan's head as he sat in that Downing Street meeting:

> How am I going to say to this girl that this is who I have met today in the role I have, and when I went home that evening, that's who I went round to see.

Every war leaves its scars, and this is one of them—a human story behind a political and policing story, something that gives us a little insight into the challenges of peace-making. It is not easy, and some are asked to do much more than others. Behind everything you see and hear in public, there is always another story being told.

I had something to do with Peter Sheridan being present at that Downing Street meeting. The night before, a Sunday night, I had spoken to Hugh Orde. He was in London with his Director of Media and Public Relations, Sinead McSweeney, and the story had broken in Ireland of the talks planned for the following day, at which Sinn Fein would be represented by Adams, McGuinness and Gerry Kelly. If I remember it correctly, I called McSweeney on her phone and she asked me to have a chat with Orde. We discussed the items he wanted to talk about the following day. He planned to link the question of republican support for policing to the issue of demilitarisation. He was going to argue that his officers needed to feel confident and safe on the ground, and that if that could be achieved, they could then patrol without Army support and the watchtowers on the hills of South Armagh could be decommissioned. He made the point that republican support for policing had to be clear, that 'they [couldn't] continue to be indifferent', and that once the IRA had left the stage, the demilitarisation process could be expedited. He told me he was trying to get someone else over to London to accompany him, and I mentioned Peter Sheridan's name. Sheridan was then Assistant Chief Constable with operational responsibility in rural areas, including South Armagh, where the controversy about the Army's watchtowers was raging. Sheridan travelled first thing Monday morning to be present at the Downing Street meeting. Was he concerned about the compromises that might be involved?

I was never lying out at night wondering who I could shoot and kill, bomb, with a mask on me, wondering what I could do, and nor was I part of anybody that discussed that or thought about that. So, I was always confident that my principles never had to change, and when I was going into that room, I knew that I was coming out with the same set of principles as I had when I went into that room. Others may have had to move their principles.

Of course, Sheridan knew that meeting was about moving the peace process forward, that was the end upon which all minds needed to be focused:

> I take people, and maybe this is just my nature, as being people. I deal with people as being human beings—not as A, B and C—as paramilitaries. I deal with people as being human beings and part of myself, I suppose, is—if this helps and moves it [the process] on, I will treat people with respect, irrespective of what I think or may know about their background.

> **Rowan**: But you knew exactly who you were meeting?
> **Sheridan**: Yes.
> **Rowan**: Their backgrounds?
> **Sheridan**: Yes I did, but I was going to treat them as human beings and treat them with respect.

Gerry Kelly was also in the room that day with his IRA record, as one of a bomb team working in London, as a prisoner who had escaped and been recaptured, and as one of those republicans who grew into political leadership as the peace process developed. He could add the weight of war service to the arguments and the theoretical debates taking place within republicanism. What were his thoughts on meeting the enemy?

> We clearly had a great suspicion of each other, of motives, of what was possible, of all of that, but remember we were the

believers—we always said talk … I do think there is a military mindset that you can get into … I would argue that we were [now] out of the mindset. As you said earlier, my history has been the IRA and clearly during that period, I mean I was very proud of it, but clearly you are in a fighting mode. When you enter politics, when you enter negotiations, you have to remove yourself certainly from the fighting mode, but certainly that doesn't mean to say that all of a sudden you're compromising on everything. You're in a battle to try and get equality, to try and get a proper police service … It [the Downing Street meeting] was cordial, became, I suppose, you could describe it almost friendly, it was very good-mannered. It was all of that … I didn't think they were ogres. I knew from their point of view they thought they were doing a job. I thought they were doing it wrong, but that's beside the point. A lot of it, I thought, was political, but once you start talking then personalities actually do come into it. So, I'm not being dismissive of personalities. Clearly if you have somebody who cannot bend and is the person who is negotiating then you're in trouble. So their personalities do come into it. It was certainly cordial, quite friendly. There were one or two humorous moments—jokes and what have you across the table.

Orde, I am told, made some quip about the controversial police search of Sinn Féin's offices during the Stormontgate investigation, which highlights what I said earlier about his subtlety and how he cannot resist being mischievous. He saw the Downing Street meeting as both a breakthrough and as a signal: a breakthrough in that it ended 'the tip-toeing around each other' and a signal in that he believed the republican leadership was now setting a strategic direction:

It was very clear at that moment to me personally that this was something that was a genuine effort to move on … The point being it was clear they wanted to move into policing—strategically they'd made their decision, but it was going to be difficult [for them] … [and] difficult for my people too.

Orde received very little notice of the meeting—a call the afternoon before, while he was out walking on the beach. For him the big issues were convincing 'nine thousand cops this is a good idea' along with the civilian support staff. He had little time, just a few hours, to prepare himself and to think about what to say, both to those he was meeting and to his colleagues within his own organisation. Afterwards, sitting at the Cabinet table with Peter Sheridan and Orde, Sinead McSweeney wrote two statements—one for the media and one for the police. And as Orde emerged from what he describes as a 'deeply important and significant meeting', he was convinced he now knew where republicans were going on this issue:

> Those debates started to move on, but it was clear that it was going to be a long run and it was clear to me their big difficulty was how they managed this internally. So my approach was I adopted a fairly stand back, let them develop their situation and we would engage when asked to engage. I did not at that stage go pro-active. It would not have been clever to try and push them into a position that made it even more difficult. So on a number of occasions one had to live with some difficult situations as the charade went on.

Up to this point, republicans had tried to deal with the broad security question at that high political level of Downing Street, probably thinking it best to engage directly with the political masters of the police and the Army, rather than with the members of the enemy forces. Accordingly, the Number 10 meeting with Orde and Sheridan represented a strategic shift that forced republicans to give serious thought to the direction the process was taking. On the eve of the meeting I heard their nervousness in a conversation with Richard McAuley, one of Adams' senior aides. Republicans offer a context for everything they do, and this phone conversation just hours before the Downing Street meeting was no different. McAuley described the talks as 'a meeting with Blair, and Hugh Orde will be there'. By this stage, and privately, the IRA had made clear what it was prepared to do on decommissioning, but the issue of the British military presence remained unresolved. The necessity of meeting with Orde was the fact that he had primacy on all operational security matters; the Army's role was in support of the police. As McAuley said: 'The Brits—both Powell and Blair—have been saying to us that operational decisions are up to Orde.' However, he went on, 'There will be no discussion with Orde on policing. A lot of our people are going to be very, very, nervous.'

There were some things they did not talk about during that London meeting, but they were thinking them, privately. Orde told me he thought it interesting 'how comfortable Sinn Féin were in Number 10—just an observation, very comfortable.' Gerry Kelly believes the Chief Constable had been waiting for this moment—his moment—to find a way into the talks, that he wanted his place and his part in them:

> Orde was looking to be in negotiations. His negotiation wasn't just with us. His negotiation was with his [political] masters. He wanted to be in it. He wanted to have the power to be able to say, 'okay, well, we will look at that, and we'll try and do that'.

I suggested to Kelly that this was all part of Orde's 'operational responsibility' on security matters, that it was he who would decide—in consultation with others in the police and Army—when military patrolling would stop, when troop numbers would be reduced, when bases were closed and military watchtowers taken off the hills of South Armagh.

If he had been dealing simply on operational capability, he would have closed them down [a range of bases and towers] well before the negotiations. He held onto them. Now, maybe he was asked—I doubt it, and I would say he would deny that he was asked to hold onto them. But he himself, it became very obvious to me—he might disagree with all of this—but it became very obvious to me that he had them sitting in his back pocket ready [for the negotiation that was now happening in Downing Street]. But it still comes back to this, 'I'm just a simple cop'. He certainly isn't.

On the contrary, Kelly considers Orde to be very political:

He has always said that he is only a cop, which nobody believes. First of all I don't believe that there is such a thing as an apolitical person, especially not when you are in such a job … I think it is a bit of a myth, but saying I'm a simple cop doesn't wash with anybody. He has made interventions, which are clearly highly political, and he makes those judgments. I think he's made some bad judgments—some good judgments, but that's true of anybody.

This was, I suppose, all part of the sizing up, trying to make judgments, trying to decide where this talking would, or could, lead. The political achievement was the fact of all these people being in the one room together. That first meeting brought together those who would have to move others, gave them that chance to sound each other out and to begin, very slowly, to develop the relationships, the trust and the understanding that would be necessary when the big decisions had to be made further down the road. In the measured steps taken by republicans, participation in policing came later—more than two years after that Downing Street meeting of November 2004 and after the IRA decisions to end the armed campaign and to decommission. Nonetheless, that meeting showed that a new possibility was on the table, one that could lead to peace, and in this lay its true significance, regardless of what was achieved on a practical level that day. In themselves, each was a significant initiative and as such had to be taken at a careful pace.

The discussions taking place in 2004 would be at the heart of the arrangements agreed in early 2007. Paisley's party made a resolution on policing an essential prerequisite to any deal, which forced the issue along. But there was more to it than that. The republican community needed policing, Adams would say wanted policing. The IRA's particular brand of 'policing', or street justice, was no longer viable and would no longer be tolerated. So, this was a bridge republicans had to cross. Come what may, Adams would have to persuade the IRA, the Sinn Féin party and the broader republican community that policing had changed, that the bridge could be crossed. In this, he needed the help of those in positions of authority in policing and politics. We could see that this was what was happening because the same trends and patterns were there: the intense internal discussions, the key republican voices speaking up, the IRA publicly showing itself to be on side with Adams and McGuinness. There were dissident voices, but they were being subdued day by day. It was obvious that Adams and McGuinness were winning the debate, and would win it outright when it came to a vote.

I thought there was a huge signal in an interview I did with Gerry Kelly in September 2006, which was published in the *Belfast Telegraph*. It was not so much what he said, but how he said it. The interview took place in the party's offices on the Falls Road on Tuesday 19 September 2006 and ran the following day, front page and inside. Before 7.00am on the morning of publication I talked it over again with Gerry Kelly on the telephone. By now, this process was getting somewhere and policing was its biggest issue, so I wanted to be absolutely sure that I was presenting his view—the leadership's view—accurately.

In that early morning conversation, Kelly told me the interview would 'cause a little ruction', but that what I read to him was 'dead on', meaning it was accurate. The 'little ruction' would be with republicans, who were being prepared for the next step. While it was part of Kelly's remit to be mindful of that reaction, he also had to choose words that pushed the boat out and set the course for the new direction. There are times when every word can be a possible landmine and a very delicate balance is required to put across a message safely. Gerry Kelly has worked with bombs and words; he knows the dangers inherent in both.

The words he chose to use in that interview were very convincing. Yes, there was a set pre-context that was necessary before changes could be wrought. The political institutions would have to be restored, which meant Paisley agreeing to power-sharing. The responsibility for policing and justice matters would have to move from British ministers to locally elected politicians in a new department. Plus, there were things that had to be worked out concerning the role of MI5 in the North in relation to police accountability. Kelly explained that he was 'futuring', and with hindsight we now know that he was 'short-futuring'. He acknowledged the 'massive changes' that had taken place within policing since the days of the RUC, and made clear that if the right circumstances were created, republican participation in policing would be 'full-bodied':

I've never taken the position that everyone—even in the RUC—was bad, neither do I accept that there was only a few bad apples. I think you had a systemised approach. It [the RUC] was certainly the frontline troops of unionist rule, and I think that we have made massive changes to that. I think we have some way [still] to go.

In all this language, I could hear that Kelly was telling me something important and telling me for a particular reason—it was to get the message across to a much wider audience than just republicans; he wanted the DUP to hear this.

> You are talking about the full package. You are talking about having achieved a new beginning to policing, then being full-bodied behind it. I think that we have proved ourselves in the past, that when we have said we will do something, and we achieve that goal, then we go for it.

I knew that the republican decision on policing would be taken at the Sinn Féin Special Árd Fheis, and I asked Kelly how quickly that could be called, in the right circumstances. 'Weeks rather than months,' was his response.

This is how I finished that report for the *Belfast Telegraph*:

> The reading between the lines in all of this is that there is a preparation, circumstances allowing, for the next big republican step in this process. Gerry Kelly, who in an IRA role had an active part in a long war, is now part of the Sinn Féin management team that is moving republicans in a new and different direction. It is a further confirmation that the IRA war is over—that the shooting of police officers or anyone else is finished, and that is what is so hugely significant about this possible—even probable—next step. "We are very, very, aware that this (policing) is the biggest obstacle that we will have to overcome in our peace strategy and our political strategy," Gerry Kelly says. But republicans are getting ready to climb over that obstacle. It depends on Ian Paisley and power sharing and on an agreement with the DUP on a policing process and future that could do more for peace than the ceasefires and all of the decommissioning and all of the words of the IRA a year ago.

That was 20 September 2006. The headline on the *Telegraph* editorial the following day was: 'Sinn Féin prepares for seismic shift'. The Special Árd Fheis took place on 28 January 2007, just four months later. That is what I meant about 'short-futuring': Kelly said it and then it began to happen, quickly and decisively. Twenty days after the Kelly interview we saw more of the play towards policing. The venue was Belfast's Europa Hotel and the date was 10 October—the eve of political negotiations at St Andrews, in Scotland, which would give us a better idea of the overall political direction and mood. The presence of key IRA individuals in the audience that night spoke for itself, proclaiming in no uncertain terms that the organisation was standing with Adams.

I was in the Europa that night and the following day the *Belfast Telegraph* published my article on the proceedings. I want to include it here as an observation at that time and as an indication of what was developing across the broad Republican movement. The headline read, 'In hotel regularly blitzed by IRA, republicans prepare to do a deal', and under that headline I wrote the following:

It was one of those occasions—one of those speeches—when the words were not nearly as important as what was going on around them. Indeed, it was a night for watching as much as listening—a night for assessing the body language, a night when republicans filled one of the biggest rooms in Belfast's Europa Hotel. How many times did the IRA target that place in those days of "war" and "Brits Out"—in those days when the guns and bombs were loud? Too many times—many more times than the fingers on both hands. But times, and thinking, and doing have changed.

Last night was one of those Sinn Féin setpieces—an Adams speech, a hunger strike film, a couple of songs, the odd joke from Gerry, and a chance to show off one or two new and young faces—faces that will figure prominently in Dublin and Donegal in the next Irish election. And all of this on the eve of St Andrews—those talks that begin today and that are about shaping the political tomorrow, the talks that are about two 'Ps' and a 'Prod'—power sharing, policing and Paisley. 'End British Direct Rule!!!' were the words on the republican banner inside the big room in the Europa. How the message is changing, and how the political targets are being adjusted. Yes, the big goal, the big aim, the big thing, is still a united Ireland; but ending direct rule, getting the Executive back, getting into government with Ian Paisley, is more than enough to be getting on with for now and for the foreseeable future. It is, in the political circumstances of today, more realistic, more achievable—the most that can be hoped for. Last night was never going to be about Adams and Sinn Féin declaring their hand before Scotland. We were never going to be told in precise terms what republicans are thinking about and what they are prepared to do on policing—but there is a preparation going on, a conditioning, a getting ready for the next big decision and compromise in this process. And on the eve of St Andrews, Adams was saying some of the right things.

"Republicans are quite rightly opposed to criminality of all kinds," he told his audience. "Those who profit from crime have to be effectively challenged and put out of business." "Our support for policing and law and order is not a response to unionist demands," he said. "Neither is it a tradeable commodity to be retained or given away as part of a deal."

But this issue—republican support for and participation in policing—is absolutely crucial if the political deal is to be done. It is why republicans are talking so much about it—talking the specifics among the key negotiators, and talking more generally to audiences like the one assembled last night. And those who are listening can hear the preparation being done. They can see where this is going. They know what it means. They don't need a dictionary to understand. After the ceasefires, the decommissioning and the ending of the armed campaign, this is the next big compromise. Significant IRA figures helped fill that room in the Europa last night—men who were jail leaders in the Maze, the man who read the statement ending the armed campaign, the man sent to jail for the Shankill bombing, men who were on the hunger strikes of '80 and '81 and men whose names have been linked to this, that and the other. Indeed one of those former jail leaders—the last jail leader in the H Blocks, Jim McVeigh—spoke the opening words of the evening and sat at the top table with Adams and the others. No one blinked an eye as the Sinn Féin president talked through the policing issue and said what he had to say on criminality. No one raised a voice in anger. No one walked out. They applauded, and in that applause they were telling Adams and the other senior party negotiators that they had their confidence and their support to do whatever has to be done in St Andrews and in whatever talking might follow. The senior police officer who told this newspaper yesterday that if the DUP do the deal on power sharing, then the 'Shinners' will do the deal on policing, is absolutely right. If you were watching and listening closely last night, you could see and hear it—hear it in those coaxing and conditioning words of Adams, and see it in the audience. They know what is coming next. If last night was anything to go by, then republicans seem comfortable, even confident, about all of this and where it is leading. They are ready for the deal, even if the deal means they have to do policing.

Politically, Ian Paisley Junior became a much more significant figure during this phase of the negotiations. He handled much of the detail on his father's behalf and in the deal-making and Executive that followed, the Paisleys would work alongside

Martin McGuinness and Gerry Kelly. That was the situation for about a year. In all the talking that made that incredible political leap possible, Paisley Junior described policing, meaning republican support for policing, as '*the* negotiating point of that process'. He described it as 'the objective that *had* to be achieved':

And if you just put it in any sort of context—here we have an organisation that for thirty years described Northern Ireland as a failed political entity, that legitimised the murder of police officers—Crown Forces, and now was prepared to, not only support and become Crown ministers, not only to support and endorse and write British law, but was prepared to support and endorse by way of a pledge or an oath, the Crown Forces. Now, if people don't see that as a U-turn, to be pejorative, don't see it as a significant concession to unionism, a concession to democracy, the thing that we have been asking for, then they are blind and want to be blind … At any point in the late seventies, early eighties … if someone had said, 'Look you can get republicans to come into a Northern Ireland parliament, you can get them to sign up to a partitionist settlement, you can get them not only to sign up to that but to sign up to the Crown Forces and support them and as well as that the cherry on top, Ian Paisley is practically your de facto Prime Minister—[and] the arms question [is] out of the way'. They would have broken your arm for that deal, but wouldn't have believed it was possible.

This was Paisley Junior speaking in October 2007 and he will, of course, argue this from his own political perspective. This analysis justifies the DUP's journey from the slogan of 'Smash Sinn Féin' to the new reality of sharing power not just with republicans but with Martin McGuinness, the man so closely identified with the IRA's war. In Paisley's commentary there is no mention of how the RUC was turned inside-out and upside-down in a process of far-reaching reforms, no mention of how it was forced off the stage to join the Ulster Defence Regiment in the pages of history, no mention of an unique recruitment programme to give better balance to the religious make-up of the PSNI and no mention of all the scrutiny that now exists, including the many powers granted to the office of the Police Ombudsman. The Force that policed during the war has changed utterly. That is the side missing from Paisley's version of the story. But regardless of the terms in which the narrative is couched, there can be no doubting the significance he and his colleagues place on the republican move into policing, that it was *the* dealmaker that made everything and so much possible:

It became possible, and only because the fact we were prepared to dig in our heels on that policing issue. And I think digging in on that issue paid huge significant dividends. And I'm not going to be behind the door on this. I think in terms of the ideological war, because there was a physical war, there was a war-war going on, but there was an ideological war going on on this island. In terms of the ideological war, unionism has proved to be, in the final analysis, the predominant ideology, because it has turned round and said, the Union remains, British law being made by British ministers even though they're Catholics, republicans, nationalists, whatever, and everyone on the same footing in terms of law and order and policing. And now we have the miracle, which is how the First Minister described it, the miracle of Sinn Féin asking for more policing on the streets of west Belfast— not special policing, not different policing, just the police to get in there and solve policing problems. That is a seismic change that is worth celebrating for everyone. And I don't want to use this to rub salt into the wounds … It is a fact that that is what has happened in terms of ideology, and in terms of on the ground, and I think that some recognition of that will say, again in the final analysis, what doctrine, what ideology, what practice on the ground, actually dominated here at the end of the day, and I believe it was unionism.

To make possible the political era of Paisley and McGuinness, the two sides had to travel a significant distance to meet each other. When the Northern Ireland Executive came to be formed, the IRA Army Council was still in place, is still in place, but its remit was no longer to organise and fight a war, instead it was to manage the transition into peace. On the republican side, orders and a direction had to be given. Therefore, before Sinn Féin convened its Special Árd Fheis in Dublin, the IRA met in a General Army Convention that was held in secret on Friday and Saturday, 26 and 27 January 2007. What happened over that weekend is described in the British intelligence community as the 'landmark event', the 'pivotal moment' in the new approach of the Provisional movement. This was *the* moment, *the* event and *the* decision that ended the war. If you were to ask in that intelligence community about Castlereagh and Stormontgate, you would be told that they were 'pre-watershed'. In other words, they are in the past. The present is now being judged on the decision taken over that weekend in January 2007, and the ensuing directive that changed everything. The IRA agreed to let Adams and McGuinness run with this and once that happened, Paisley and the DUP had no choice but to say yes. They were in a corner. At every level, political, intelligence and security, the British knew that the IRA's war was finished, and that mattered more than anything else. When you listen to Martin McGuinness now, you know that it is finished, that he and his colleagues are in a new place:

The way I look at policing is that there had been much wrong with policing in the north of Ireland since the foundation of the northern state—effectively the police were seen as a military wing of unionism. The big challenge for us is to bring about a situation where the police are de-politicised, where they are not the military arm of anybody, that they are there to support the community and to provide sane and sensible policing for the benefit of everyone. At the same time whenever I see police men and I see them in uniform there is an instinctive thing in you, I have been arrested, I have been assaulted in interrogation centres, I've had my home searched. So, there is an instinctive thing to be anti, but it has to be part of a bigger plan. And these people who were in the police in the past, the vast majority of them were from the unionist community, they were supportive of the unionist political parties, but they live here just like me. I'm beginning to get irritated even with myself when I use [the term] 'both sides of the community'. I no longer see both sides of the community. We are one community, and within it there are people who think differently, and that's all right … So the changes that have taken place in terms of policing, much of it as the result of the negotiations that Sinn Féin have been involved in, have brought us to a point where we can move forward now decisively to support the police and to do it in a way that will bring huge benefits for all of the people that we represent. I think we can bring an end to the political policing that has afflicted us for far too long.

If you ask McGuinness to compare the policing of Orde and the PSNI with that of Flanagan and the RUC, he replies quickly:

They are only different because we have, through negotiations, brought about the difference. We've made it different, absolutely. And I also think that what we can't rule out of this is that there are people within the police who recognise the huge mistakes of the past and who don't want to be part of repeating those mistakes in the future. So, it is our job to

work with those people to make this a better place and that's
what we are very, very determined to do.

Those words described the change that has been effected not just
within policing but across Northern Irish society. It wasn't an easy
feat, not at all. The republican leadership had to bring people
from seeing the RUC as the opponent in a necessary war to seeing
the PSNI as their police service. Sir Hugh Orde is under no illusion
as to what obstacles had to be overcome in order to achieve this:

> There are huge parallels in how you move an organisation—
> change management. They [republicans] were going through
> their Patten ... The essence was that was what they were doing
> ... It was very well managed ... Sinn Féin is organised. They
> told me it was going to be difficult. You saw the way it played
> itself. They clearly had spent a lot of time—they put a lot of
> effort I think into talking the rank and file through it, in the
> same way that we put a lot of effort into making sure our
> people knew what was going on. They clearly had an effective
> communications strategy, and it clearly was doing what I do
> now. The only way you get to your people is talk to your
> people ... It's face-to-face stuff ... You've got to use people with
> credibility. The world sort of moves on and my people routine-
> ly, I mean it is strange, my people routinely speak to IRA people
> out there—the guy I met in one of our District Command
> Units, the sergeant, the inspector, the local PIRA commander of
> the past talking about community policing ... It's strange
> alliances, but to get to that stage the big leaders had to take big
> risks ... and it must have been a rocky ride. It's like my world.
> Some of the parts of my organisation are easier than others.

The vote at the Special Árd Fheis was overwhelmingly in
support of the leadership motion (see Appendix 4), but this
story was bigger than a show of hands—the conference was

only part of the picture. There was, as always, an off-stage element, a series of private discussions and meetings that formed the backdrop to the final vote. Sinn Féin's stance on this issue depended on what the IRA would allow. Its voices had to be heard and they were heard in the debate, including those of Bobby Storey, Padraic Wilson and Sean Murray alongside those of Adams, McGuinness and Kelly. All of this was part of the strategy behind the deal with Paisley. It was a drive to remove from him any reason for saying no and to push him ever closer to having to say yes. At this point, the policing issue was going to make or break the deal, and it made it by making it impossible for Paisley to walk away. The war was over and so too were the politics of 'never' and 'no'. Adams and McGuinness had delivered their part; Orde had to deliver his.

> My big concern, leading this organisation [the PSNI], bearing in mind its history, [was] there were clearly going to be concerns. So, we did have a strategy to deal with that, and it was around information and describing what we were doing. I sent an email to the whole organisation explaining why this was the right way to move—obviously the Patten imperative, and the commonsense imperative and the long-term future of Northern Ireland imperative. So, it was very clear it was something [we had] to do, [but] it didn't make it easy.

Orde received quite a few emails in reply to his, the majority of which understood the reasons for the engagement with republicans. People saw it as a way out of the war. Older officers with long years of service were telling the Chief Constable that if it meant their children would not have to live through what they had experienced, then 'yeah, it makes sense. We can understand it.'

> So, managing our organisation was not as difficult as I thought it would be, and hasn't been since. I think what it did

do was it opened up in most places an increasing engagement [between the police and the republican community].

None of this is to suggest a cosy relationship between the police and the republican community—far from it. Given all that has happened, it is going to take time for this to take root and grow. The positive signs are there, however, as Gerry Kelly sees it:

> Once you get through the first introductions of being friendly and shaking hands and doing all of that, then when you have a row, you know that it's a political row as opposed to a personal row. And I do think it's important in those circumstances that it's made clear, and by making clear I don't mean you have to say it's not personal, but I do think it became very obvious to them and to us that this is not an issue of personalities. This is an issue of trying to get something sorted out.

While this new relationship is nowhere near perfect, things are 'infinitely better' according to Assistant Chief Constable Peter Sheridan. There is a 'but', however. Sheridan knows it will take time for the republican decision that marked the strategic shift in direction and policy to work its way down to the ground:

> The relationship between a lot of police officers and Sinn Féin is still nowhere near where it should be and will be in the future, and that is going to take considerable time yet.

That is absolutely right. However, the importance in all of this is that politically it created a situation where, within months, Paisley would be able to be in the same room as Adams and then, just weeks later, in government with Martin McGuinness. The Paisley–Provo deal was close to being made now, and it was in that once-unthinkable political link that we finally got confirmation that the war was truly over.

Chapter 6

Paisley: A journey through Never and No

There must be republicans and nationalists out there, who say, 'How can he stand doing business with that man Paisley?' ... And vice-versa ... It's no secret ... that Martin McGuinness is loathed within unionism. But you're right, the characters who have to lead, and the arrangements that we have now in place, require strong dominant personalities that can carry that sort of thing off despite that mutual feeling on each side.
(IAN PAISLEY JUNIOR SPEAKING IN OCTOBER 2007.)

His mind struggle would always have been, am I doing what my conscience tells me, am I doing right, am I selling out, and this is very important—this selling out business is very important, am I selling out? I give credit to Paisley for the road that he has travelled.

The silence of opposition is thunderous. The people are happy with it—they are happy with the outcome ... But in the peculiarity of Northern Ireland it was amazing—it was amazing.

I believe that Paisley became very practical when-ever Peter Robinson, whom I believe is one of the main cutting edges that led the DUP to be where they are today. He's very, very, shrewd—good politician. There was only one better politician in Stormont, and I'm not including David Ervine here, [it] was Seamus

Mallon—incisive, very, very good, and Robinson is
exactly the same. And Robinson has helped to bring
Paisley along.
(FORMER UVF LEADER GUSTY SPENCE COMMENTING
ON IAN PAISLEY DOING BUSINESS WITH MARTIN
McGUINNESS.)

I appreciate how big a step it was for Ian Paisley, I
also appreciate how difficult it was for Ian Paisley,
I also appreciate that there's a lot of pain associated
with all of that. But I think that people also have to
accept that it is also very difficult for us given our
view of Ian Paisley over the course of all of his adult
political life, and our view of his contribution to the
history of the northern state over the course of all of
that period.

Ian Paisley and I meet, as we did do in the course
of this week, the Chinese Ambassador, the Russian
Ambassador, we've met people from all over the
world who've come here. And I've put it like this—
If they want to come into this room or Ian's room
and put their finger in the wound, that's not an apt
description, but it is almost like people are
[Doubting] Thomas, and unless they see Ian Paisley
and I together speaking with them and speaking to
each other, then they find it very, very difficult to
believe. People, understandably, are asking, is this
true, is this real, is this happening? But it's true, it is
real, it is happening, and I believe he is as dedicated
to making this work as I am, and I believe that he
believes I am as dedicated to making it work as he is.
(MARTIN McGUINNESS COMMENTING ON IAN
PAISLEY'S STEP INTO GOVERNMENT WITH SINN
FÉIN.)

Politically, I suppose in a very simplistic way, you could say, yes, in a way it is the unthinkable. On the other hand, so often in these processes it is the people who were on the outside who in the end have the capacity to deliver and to make the unthinkable possible. And both of these were skilled operators who earned their spurs in their own particular contexts and have therefore a degree of credibility with people, but also had the political skill to find their way through the maze, and maybe as well to understand when it was time to fish and when it was time to cut bait.
(FORMER ASSEMBLY SPEAKER LORD ALDERDICE ON
THE PAISLEY–McGUINNESS GOVERNMENT.)

He is an extraordinary politician with an intuitive feel for the pulse of the ordinary unionist man and woman, and they were telling him do the deal—do it Big Man. That's what he kept saying to me … He felt very confident that he could carry the people.
(FORMER NORTHERN IRELAND SECRETARY OF STATE
PETER HAIN ON IAN PAISLEY SAYING YES.)

Stormont, 26 March 2007: the image that was being transmitted on my television screen was historic in every way: Ian Paisley and Gerry Adams sitting in the same room in Stormont, reading from prepared scripts, telling us they had agreed a way forward. Sitting there, watching the action unfold, I couldn't help thinking that anything is possible in politics. The momentum of a peace process can change everything, and everyone.

It has certainly changed Ian Paisley, the man who will long be associated with the words 'never' and 'no'. Paisley represented the last trench, the place of final resistance. He was the man who stood in the way of everything, who could block the route of all that was meant to flow from the Good Friday Agreement. Remember the Paisley of 'smash Sinn Féin' and of 'sackcloth and ashes' and 'over our dead bodies'? Remember the Paisley of the Third Force and Ulster Resistance? Remember the Paisley of the City Hall rally of the mid-1980s, veins bulging in his neck as he shouted with venom, 'Never, Never, Never'? When one remembers that Paisley, the Paisley sitting at the table with Adams and McGuinness seems almost unfathomable. What changed him so utterly?

Paisley had been thinking the unthinkable for some time, but he had to find a way to that new beginning through the debris of all he had said in the past. How would he, how could he, make the journey from No to Yes? We watched his struggle, as he tried to come to terms with what he knew he had to do, the political inevitability of this new situation. He was given help— from the Provos and the Prods, from the the IRA and the loyal- ists—who strove to create the circumstances that would make possible this deal of all deals.

Occasionally, Gerry Adams would have spoken to David Ervine to ask his advice before addressing the unionist/loyalist community. Ervine told me that it was he who suggested to Adams that he ask Paisley if *his* war was over. That's quite a remarkable statement. It was Ervine, from his loyalist back- ground, accepting that the IRA war was over and urging Adams to challenge Paisley to step up and make the deal. He was saying something else, too: that this time, unlike a previous time, the loyalists would not stand in the way of a power-sharing arrangement. Indeed, it was not just Ervine who was saying this. The UVF also said it, in interviews with me in April and August 2006. At base, Paisley's change of tack was made possible by the IRA declaring an end to its war and confirming that promise through acts of decommissioning.

Perhaps, what was crucial to this deal, though, more than

anything else, was the republican endorsement of policing. Paisley could argue that he had achieved more than Trimble, that he had gotten more out of the IRA than any other unionist leader before him. But while the republicans did move first— the ending of the armed campaign, the decommissioning, the policing decision—they knew what they were doing. And while there was a risk attached to those steps they took, it was not as great as many might think. A source from inside Adams' kitchen Cabinet tells how it worked:

> We had a strategic goal since 2004—from at least 2004—to close down all the other options, and to leave the DUP with one choice: either go for it or collapse everything and be publicly seen as the villain of the peace.

I believe there have been contacts between Sinn Féin and the DUP dating back to the 2004 negotiations. The contacts were facilitated first by a journalist and then by a Protestant churchman, who has had other important roles in the peace process. It meant that inside Adams' kitchen Cabinet there was at least an understanding of some of the thinking within the DUP. That party has consistently denied such contacts. For republicans, the central question always was about Paisley: would he, could he, come to share power and government with McGuinness? For a long time Danny Morrison, the republican strategist of the pre-ceasefire years, doubted that the old man of the DUP could make that journey:

> I got Paisley wrong. I was saying this man cannot [do a deal with republicans]. It means he is repudiating everything he did. What was the point of the '77 strike? What was the point of the Third Force? What was the point of him blocking the Armagh civil rights march in November 1968?

The struggle to believe in these new possibilities was shared by the whole community, from politicians to the people on the streets. For those sitting at the negotiating table, it was very difficult to accept and process the information now being presented. As Ian Paisley Junior remarks:

> The DUP was serious when it was saying things like, we will accept a power-sharing arrangement, we will accept a deal that will include nationalists, republicans, whatever, but these are the terms. They of course didn't believe us that we would accept them at any price.

Quite simply, for both sides the new language of negotiation was very hard to come to terms with. What the DUP was saying now was just so far removed from everything that had gone before. Paisley junior will still tell you that Trimble 'jumped too soon', that 'he didn't push them [republicans] as hard as he should have done on the criminality and policing' and that 'he took them on trust', pointing out that:

> We at no point have had to take Sinn Féin on trust, and that is the subtle but very, very important difference.

One can make this argument about jumping too soon, but in the working of this process someone had to make the first move. Indeed, it was the hardest role to be the one to take that step because of the uncertainty, the unnerving fact that nothing was guaranteed. Trimble did it with loyalist cover: the political representatives of the UDA and the UVF entered the talks with him and played a part in developing the Good Friday Agreement. Trimble opened unionist minds to new thinking and new realities, which meant that when it came to Paisley's turn, people had at least had time to think about it and come to terms with what it meant. The 'jumping too soon' was actually being brave enough to take the first step, but the nature of the process meant that things couldn't happen quickly nor on one person's or side's terms. Paisley demanded things he never got—decommissioning photographs, a witness at the decommissioning, the return of the Northern Bank money, the IRA Army Council stood down. But these things have now been conveniently forgotten. This has been a slow, piecemeal process and Trimble got a lot of it done; that enabled Paisley to step in when the weight that had to be shouldered was not as heavy.

This has been a feature of the process—that it tends to forget about people as it surges forward. However, David Trimble's contribution should not be forgotten or diminished. He shouldered the political weight when it was at its heaviest, when the thorny issues of the RUC, prisoner release, republicans in government and IRA arms all still remained to be resolved. Not only did he open unionist minds to the possibilities ahead, he also showed republicans what all of this change would mean. Trimble could be the most awkward, difficult and infuriating man, someone who always seemed to know best. But regardless of his own weaknesses, he got this process started and put it on the right road. That took political courage and vision, as well as huge personal stamina and commitment. It was, I think it's fair to say, a leap of faith rather than a 'jumping too soon'.

Paisley Junior, understandably, chooses to concentrate on the achievements of his father and his party, on the making of the new government with Paisley and McGuinness after the ending of war, the decommissioning and the decision on policing. The process is in a different place now and in a new phase. Each side points to its negotiating achievements. We are at the beginning of new relationships. Speaking in October 2007, Paisley Junior accepted that it would take time for trust to grow:

The point of the Rubicon is it's … the point of no going back. No matter what they want to do, there is no going back. For credibility reasons, they can't go back. For political reasons, they can't go back. Within their own community, they can't go back. So whether they like it or not the trajectory is one way … I think that Sinn Féin have recognised that this is a new dispensation, this is a change, and the final solution looks like this. Now, take the personalities out of this—the big personalities on each side—and no one can see a significantly different solution … There will be tweaks here and there … Maybe we'll get to the point where trust comes into the equation, but at the moment we have politics without trust, but we've got politics. That's the important thing … So we have the politics without trust. We'll move at some point to where trust comes into the equation, but all I'm saying is trust is not necessary at this point.

On the republican side, they are now doing business with the DUP. Their strategic goal in negotiations was to remove all excuses from the DUP repertoire, leaving them with 'yes' as the only option. That has brought them to this position, where old opponents are now partners in government. McGuinness is clear on how this has come to pass:

I think that's a crude way to put it—removing their excuses. More importantly for me throughout all of that process was to create circumstances which would see the Democratic Unionist Party, no matter how unrealistic the public may have thought that would have been, but see the Democratic Unionist Party recognise that, as they had said consistently, that they were committed devolutionists, and it was clear to me had an antipathy towards being told what to do by British Government direct rule ministers, that they would be brought to a point as a result of the combined efforts of everyone, not least the contributions that we would make within republicanism, to a point where they would accept that if they wanted into government, then they had one big reality to face—that the only way into government was alongside Sinn Féin. And, therefore they would then have to begin a thought process within their party, that they had to begin the process of making that happen albeit on whatever terms they set out for themselves.

McGuinness had figured it out: there was only one way through all of this, and republicans could clear that path for Paisley. That was what they realised, and that was what they did, very effectively. In the end, the DUP entered government; the IRA had not won or lost the military fight; and politically Sinn Féin had not been smashed.

Even now, Paisley Junior prefers to speak about these things in matter-of-fact terms, avoiding the mental struggles and emotions that were undoubtedly part of it. His approach is to concentrate on the final pieces of the jigsaw, and, I think, almost to block out much of the rest of the picture. He will colour in those bits he is comfortable with, but leaves out much else. It is easier that way because it's less complicated to describe the republican journey, rather than the Paisley one. In order to line up past and present, the Paisley script has to stick to a particular viewpoint:

We outlined seven key principles. Those key principles, looking at them with hindsight for anyone who wasn't on the same page as us, it was pretty clear to see that if certain things happened where this process was going to end up. And throughout all that period the NIO were constantly at us and all their runners and movers [were saying], 'But you guys aren't serious. Does that really mean that there will be a government that will include these people?' And we spelt out what the terms and conditions were. It was up to others to then test us. Now we were tested throughout that period and

I think we were not found wanting, but it was up to others to then come up to that mark. And, I think fair dos to the DUP. We said what we would do, when it happened, even against some of our harder elements, we went on ahead and did what we had to do. We believe in that contract. There's the position. You come up to that mark, [and] you're in. That's where we got to … law and order was crucial.

'Law and order' means the republican decision on policing, and it was this that made everything else possible and allowed Paisley to cross his Rubicon. For every move that one side made, moves were demanded in response from the other. There was no winning for Paisley or for the Provos; compromises were sought and demanded on both sides. This was how the process haltingly wound its way to its current destination. And who knows if this is the political endgame—who would say that with any confidence?

For decades, Gusty Spence has watched those twists and turns of the Paisley journey. He talks about those mind games and emotional struggles, Paisley's battle with his conscience, the questioning about 'selling out', the constant wondering: 'am I doing the right thing?' And he talks, too, about the influence of Peter Robinson, a politician he places alongside Seamus Mallon in terms of ability, and how he 'helped bring Paisley along' by making him 'very practical'. Spence can regard all this with a dispassionate eye, and also from the position of understanding the republican mind probably better than any unionist politician. Paisley's main political achievement, Spence will tell you, was 'to be the leader of the unionist people', and while his coming to government with Martin McGuinness may well have been 'amazing', especially 'in the peculiarity of Northern Ireland', Spence will also tell you that 'it was inevitable':

It could have been Trimble. It could have been Paisley. In fairness, Trimble and Hume were the forerunners.

But he believes Trimble and his colleagues underestimated the increasing strength and popularity of the DUP and Sinn Féin. When those two parties took the lead political roles in 2003, the endpoint in their journeys became 'inevitable':

> To me, whenever you have two extremes coming together, it is strange, because people have fought and died and there were all types of things which had happened in the past. But the strangeness was the inevitability … These things, they happen all the time, but in the peculiarity of Northern Ireland, it was amazing—it was amazing.
>
> Republicanism has still maintained its integrity. Paisley has still maintained his integrity.

What Spence means is that republicans have not given up on the goal, i.e. they will continue to pursue a United Ireland, but from within a political process rather than a war:

> That's what Sinn Féin/republicanism will attempt to do— broaden the empire towards that goal, a chip here and a chop there.

And all the while Paisley could point to the Union being safe and the principle of consent accepted by republicans:

> The silence of opposition is thunderous. The people are happy with it—they're happy with the outcome.

Nonetheless, Paisley's struggle in reaching that outcome was clear in the words he spoke on 12 July 2006—a year after the IRA had formally ended its armed campaign. That speech sounded like the bad old days, the old Paisley, the politician and the man who would never bend. At this stage the negotiation process was working towards a November deadline, but Paisley's language and message was: 'over our dead bodies'. I wrote about it in the *Belfast Telegraph* under the headline: 'The IRA has gone away, but does Paisley care?'

I suppose it is best described as a kind of "sackcloth and ashes" moment part two. The setting was the field in Portrush on that day of all days for Protestant Ulster—the twelfth of July. Ian Paisley had an audience, and his seemingly uncompromising message on power sharing with "IRA/Sinn Féin" as he describes it was "over our dead bodies". His voice of over 80 years was full of the usual fire and fury. We are a year on from the IRA statement ending its armed campaign—that P O'Neill moment of last summer in which republicans "played their two big cards". They abandoned armed struggle and then moved to put their weapons beyond use. Not that many miles away from Portrush on that same twelfth of July, the IRA of 2006 was on the streets of Ardoyne, as it had been on the streets of west Belfast days earlier for the Whiterock parade. It was a presence that kept things quiet—a presence that ensured that this summer's walk through those contentious routes of the Orange marching season passed without all of the madness of the previous year. It was change that we could see and feel, that is if we wanted to. All we had to do was look—look onto those June and July streets of north and west Belfast, and we could see for ourselves the changing IRA. What a difference a year had made. "See what they can do when they want to," was what one loyalist observed, but it was to totally misread the situation. It was not that republicans wanted to accommodate marches and marchers where they are not wanted. This was the IRA of 2006 doing what had to be done—trying to protect the peace and trying to nurture whatever slim hope there is of a November deal with the man who not that many miles away was shouting out "over our dead bodies". As he shouted, many in the peace process cringed, as I'm sure did some in his own party. "It seemed to jar with everything else," was the kindest description one senior political source could make of this latest Paisley performance. A year on from the IRA initiative of last July, republicans are asking themselves, "in critical terms", what was it all about? There has been no political return, and what they see is a "pandering" to Paisley and the DUP. In 1996, the IRA response in a similar political stalemate was to bomb London, but there has been a decade of change since. "Republicans accept we are now down to absolutely political struggle without an armed campaign or the threat of an armed campaign," a source told the *Belfast Telegraph*. "While there's always a way back to those things [armed struggle], there's no desire," the veteran republican added. Read between those lines, and there is only one message. The IRA's war is over, and the loyalists will come closer to ending theirs if Ian Paisley can bring himself to the point of a political deal with Sinn Féin in November or soon thereafter. Recently, the PSNI Chief Constable Sir Hugh Orde told this newspaper that the IRA is delivering on the commitments it made last July, and just a few days ago, there were similar assessments from Secretary of State Peter Hain and the Republic's Justice Minister Michael McDowell. So for how much longer can Ian Paisley say no? Will he be able to hold to his "over our dead bodies" line when the Independent Monitoring Commission next reports in October? Are we not now at a point where we leave the issue of any continuing criminality to be dealt with by the police and the Assets Recovery Agency? Is there anyone—someone—in the DUP big enough, bold enough, to tell the party leader that the world has changed, and in it the IRA is changing? Did they not see it for themselves during those recent days of marching? The loyalist politician David Ervine says others did see it. "While this type of praise doesn't come easy, many loyalists also keeping a watching brief on the parades issue, begrudgingly were very favourably impressed by the actions of republicans ensuring calm," he says. "I have conversations in my community all the time. The war's over. If Paisley said, 'I'm doing a deal tomorrow', there wouldn't be a stone thrown in the unionist community." The Derry businessman Brendan Duddy has watched the IRA evolution over a period of many years, and has watched a hopeless situation develop into our imperfect peace. "One by one the volunteers are retiring out of active service," he says. When there was no ceasefire and when there was little hope, Duddy was the secret link between the British Government and the republican leadership. "We are very fortunate that we have the current leadership of Adams, McGuinness, Kelly and others, who have taken the steps to deliver the peace," the now Policing Board member says. "You don't have to love them, you may not even be able to abide them, but you have to recognise what is happening this day," he continues. Duddy believes that the Adams/McGuinness/Kelly leadership has "dismantled" the war, and he describes last September's acts of decommissioning as "one of the most remarkable achievements in Irish history". What he says we now need is for the peace to be "feelable"—something that can be touched, something that we know is real. He makes the observation that across the world there is a "big scarcity of people who are delivering peace". Here, at least, we have a chance. Yes, people are very sceptical when they are told that every gun has been decommissioned and that there is no centrally organised criminality. But those who know the IRA best—inside and outside that organisation—are totally convinced that the war of bombs and bullets is over. You can see and hear it for yourself—hear it in the silence of the guns, and see it on those summer marching streets in Belfast.

That article was published on 28 July 2006, some months before the republican conferences and decisions on policing and less than a year before Paisley entered government with Martin McGuinness. And yet listen to what Paisley was saying—still a part of him saying no, still capable of all that fire and fury. Gusty Spence reads Paisley well—his battle with his conscience, that internal tug-o'-war pulling him one way and then another. It was a Herculean effort that took him from the fury of No to the forward-thinking of Yes. He had no option, in the end, but to find a way to reconcile all that he had said and done in the past with what lay before him. How was he was able to do it? Because he is Ian Paisley. In the end, it was that simple. Just listen to his son, speaking in an interview recorded in October 2007:

> It can only work because of the personalities involved—certainly on our side. There is no doubt that Ian Paisley is a huge and significant personality, has got charisma and confidence in bucket loads. But as well as that I also think he's an air of doing and knowing what he's doing is the right thing to do at the right time, and he has been able to carry that off … He has the confidence of the unionist people—the wee woman up the Shankill Road, or the wee farmer in Broughshane, is with him on this. They want to see this because they trust the Big Man … He is a touchstone of what iconic unionism should be, and that's why any attack on him just falls off. It's like a hammer blow on an anvil. It means nothing. It doesn't even dent it. It doesn't mark it. Everyone used to think that Ian Paisley wasn't a leader [that] he was a follower. In other words he licked his finger and found out which way the wind was blowing and then followed the people. I always took the view that my father was a leader and is a leader, and leadership is not 'followship'. Leadership is saying, 'that's where I'm going to go, that's where I'm going to take you, these issues I can spell out to you, other issues trust me', and he traded on both—getting people to trust him and telling them straight what it would mean, and he got there.

What is apparent in those comments is more convenient forgetting and ignoring. Paisley took the leap forward because he could and because there was nowhere else to go. The republican strategic plan had ensured that. Plan A, as far as the negotiating parties were concerned, was the Paisley–McGuinness Executive, but the British and Irish Governments then started to talk about a Plan B, something that had the whiff of joint authority about it, which would naturally worry unionists. I am not sure whether Plan B was intended to push Paisley into government or to help him into government, but alongside the ending of the IRA campaign, it too served to nudge Paisley in one direction. During this crucial period Peter Hain was Secretary of State. He did a number of important things, including introducing the real issues of day-to-day politics into the debate, such as education, health, planning and water charges. He was making clear what he intended to do and, I suppose, challenging the local parties, but particularly Paisley and the DUP, to make the deal and to do better for Northern Ireland. Some of what Hain was proposing, specifically around new charges and education reforms, was highly unpopular, but he made clear that these decisions could be reversed if locally elected politicians took responsibility for them:

> I think Ian realised that for the very first time for unionism there was a downside to saying no ... For me I think actually the pressure from the people, the voters, was much, much more important. Plan B was an abstract thing. I don't know that Plan B amounted to a fantastic amount.

That, according to a senior political source, was the purpose and the design of the Hain strategy. He was pushing Paisley to say yes by making it so unpopular to say no. There was something else going on, too. Against the advice of some of his officials in the NIO, Hain took a strategic decision in July 2006 to get close to Ian Paisley Junior. The two had several one-to-one meetings at Hillsborough, usually early morning, after Paisley Junior had dropped his children to school, and in the evening. 'His party colleagues wouldn't know, but his dad would know,' was how one source put it to me.

Hain saw Paisley Junior as his father's 'gatekeeper' and therefore believed that the way to persuading and convincing Paisley Senior to do the deal was through his son. So that is where Hain's political effort began to be concentrated. 'He's very intelligent. He protects his father's back like a sort of armoured plating,' was one source's observation on Paisley Junior, and it was in this period that he was given an elevated role in the negotiating process.

One of the things Sinn Féin was trying to do—not just in this period but throughout the whole time it was negotiating at arm's length with the DUP—was to assess who had the most influence around Paisley. Was it Peter Robinson and those advisors closest to him? Was it the Church? Or was it his family that, in fact, held most sway? Others were trying to make similar assessments; Peter Hain placed his bet on Paisley Junior. Others again, however, dismissed Paisley Junior as 'a chancer', but it was clear that his father was depending on him, particularly in complex, detailed negotiations.

The key talking in 2006 took place at St Andrews in Scotland, in October. It was conceded that November was no longer a realistic deadline, but this latest negotiation set out the incremental steps that would lead to a planned March deal, 26 March to be more precise. It all hinged on the republican decision on policing, followed by a breathing period in which to assess the sincerity of any stated change in policy. The DUP wanted all of this to be linked to a formal pledge of support for the police and the courts system, and wanted to know the wording of the motion that Adams and McGuinness would take to the Sinn Féin Special Árd Fheis. This became part of the background toing and froing that was bringing everyone closer to their moments of decision.

Peter Hain recalls the behind-the-scenes manoeuvres that characterised these important negotiations:

> I remember talking to him [Paisley Senior] privately at Christmas in Hillsborough in 2005 … and he was saying to me then, 'look, I want to do this, but it has to be right'.
>
> I realised in the summer of 2006 in the lead-up to St Andrews that policing actually was *the* issue.
>
> I remember saying to the Prime Minister—this is the issue. And of course from the Sinn Féin leadership's point of view, they felt they [the IRA] had decommissioned, they had delivered an end to the war, and now they were being asked to leap over another hurdle before they knew that Ian Paisley was going to deal with them. And I kept saying to Gerry and Martin, when I had private meetings with them—he is going to deliver if you deliver. I was absolutely confident. Tony Blair was less than confident … there were hiccups, but I was clear that we were going to reach our destination—Tony, he had been at it for ten gruelling years.

Those ten gruelling years were bound to have taken their toll, and it is entirely understandable that Blair may well have been more cautious and less confident than Hain, who was relatively new to all of this. But in the relationship he was building with Paisley Junior, the Secretary of State was perhaps getting a clearer view from Hillsborough than the Prime Minister was seeing from Downing Street. Remember also that the process and its key players had bad memories of Paisley Junior—it was he who had arranged, through me, for a camera to be present so that his father's words of 'sackcloth and ashes' could be heard by a wider audience. But now, much faith and confidence was being placed directly in him. Could he be trusted to deliver?

Why should he be trusted to deliver? No doubt these questions surfaced during those final, tense moments of negotiation.

Before the deal was finally done, there would be a few more wobbles, an election and a little more time given to calm the nerves. In one last stand-off before matters were finally agreed, Hain persuaded Tony Blair to speak directly to Paisley Junior— a confirmation, I suppose, of his growing influence and status. Around his father, he was the person who now mattered most. The Paisleys would have known in the Assembly elections of March 2007 that the people wanted a local Executive, whatever its make-up. In other words, if it meant Martin McGuinness and Sinn Féin back in government, then so be it. It was the only way available to reverse some of those unpopular Hain policy decisions. The political irrelevance of dissident republicanism was seen in the results of that election. Following on from its decisions on policing and on its way to making government with Paisley, Sinn Féin won 28 seats, the DUP 36. This meant that the two parties would be the dominant forces in the new Assembly and Executive.

The St Andrews Agreement had made 26 March the day for the deal. That would slip, but not by much. Instead, that date produced the first ever joint Paisley–Adams news conference, at which the two party leaders read agreed statements. They announced 8 May 2007 as the new first day of government. Prior to this newscast the DUP and Sinn Féin had spent two days talking to each other at Stormont Castle and by telephone. But it was Monday morning, 26 March 2007, when Gerry Adams and Martin McGuinness spoke directly to Ian Paisley for the first time. McGuinness found the process smooth and easy:

> Well it wasn't difficult at all. I spent several days with Peter Robinson and Ian Paisley junior and Nigel Dodds prior to the 26th in Stormont Castle and essentially made the arrangements and done the negotiations with them as to how

the events of March 26th would be outlined for the public and for the media, who were totally unsuspecting whenever we arrived here [at Parliament Buildings]. So, the first time I ever spoke to Ian Paisley was during the course of that meeting ... I expected a continuation of the conversations that I had with his son and with Nigel Dodds and with Peter Robinson, and I expected that the agreements that we had made over the weekend would be kept and that the statements which we agreed over the weekend that Gerry and Ian Paisley would make would be kept to word for word, and that would be the beginning of a process unparalleled in the course of the history of the Northern State.

Paisley Junior described that weekend negotiation at Stormont Castle as 'businesslike', with the two parties spelling out their needs and then doing the maths and coming up with a workable equation:

I dealt straight that day. Our party dealt straight that day. There were issues which we tick-boxed off, we got and moved on. It was the most significant meeting the DUP had to take in its entire journey ... We spelt out at that meeting what had to be done and then it was fine-tuned over that weekend.

Some people think that politics is about absolutes. And the way politics is portrayed it is about absolutes in its portrayal. But the reality is it's far from absolutes. And what we'd to do was measure, well what's Sinn Féin's absolute position and what are they getting? What is our absolute position and what are we achieving? And we were able to see that we were far more in advance and at the point where our absolutes were being met and that Sinn Féin was going backwards. That was the point to do the deal. Not at the point where they would be able to advance, but the point where they were checked. And that day, whilst it was hard I think for some people in terms of actually getting there and doing it, it was checkmate against Sinn Féin to unionism, and it has been checkmate ever since.

I still wonder who he is trying to convince. Is he trying to justify the Paisley journey? Does he need to justify it? Are all those words really about reassuring himself and his father that they did the right thing? Is it as conclusive as checkmate? Has the ideological war really been won? Have republicans really suffered such a defeat at the hands of the DUP within the political negotiations and process? Or are those mind struggles still going on? Is that tug-o'-war still not decided? The St Andrews Agreement, for all its tinkering and tweaking, still walks and talks so much like the Good Friday Agreement that Paisley and the DUP opposed. And why does Martin McGuinness seem so relaxed and comfortable in this new political arrangement?

Oh, I have a completely different sense of the institutions that I'm in now—completely different. I think that we have now clearly reached the situation where we are dealing with a political leadership within unionism that isn't looking over its shoulder at anybody. So, there's no sense of insecurity on their behalf, and we certainly aren't looking over our shoulder at anybody. So we're getting on with the business of implementing the agreements that we made between us and with the governments. And I think there's overwhelming support in the community for that. So, there's a great sense of stability … What encourages me is that we all see it as part of a process, because we've all signed up to power sharing in the North. I mean Aidan McAteer's with me as my political adviser in the Department of the Office of First and Deputy First Minister, he was also my adviser in the Department of Education. His uncle led the Nationalist Party here for 15 years, during which time the only piece of legislation they got passed was the Wild Birds Act. I'm in government now with five Sinn Féin government ministers—myself and four others— and we're dealing with huge issues on an ongoing basis.

You can read into those comments an opinion that the political chessboard has opened up since the old days of Stormont and the era of unionist and one-party rule. There is no checkmate. Not anymore. We are playing a different political game now—a situation made possible by the significant compromises of more than one side. Lord Alderdice, the Speaker in that first Assembly after the Good Friday Agreement, watched the Paisley and McGuinness manoeuvres with interest:

And I think both of them would say to you that they feel that the other has made serious efforts to try to make the thing work. It is quite remarkable … I think there are some fascinating human dimensions to the whole thing, but politically, I suppose in a very simplistic way, you could say, yes, in a way it's the unthinkable. On the other hand, so often in these processes it is the people who were on the outside who in the end have the capacity to deliver and to make the unthinkable possible. And both of these were skilled operators, who earned their spurs in their own particular contexts … but also had the political skill to find their way through the maze, and maybe as well to understand when it was time to fish and when it was time to cut bait … They had the capacity both to be very tough. I mean incisively tough … and not necessarily to feel that loyalty to individual people is the ultimate value … and I think both of them have a more than grudging admiration for the other one's abilities despite deeply disagreeing.

In their respective decisions, the two men had to let some people walk away. McGuinness stood with Adams during that internal battle within the IRA in the months leading to the Good

Friday Agreement. They did not allow the dissidents, some of them in senior IRA positions, to set the course for the Republican movement. Paisley, for his part, watched Jim Allister MEP leave the party as it moved towards sharing government with Sinn Féin. In the end, the bigger picture mattered more than personal relationships.

It is galling to some people that it has come to this: the man who promised 'no' and 'never' sitting in government with a man so closely associated with the bombs and the bullets and the war of the IRA. The people decided and that is democracy. It was, after all, the people who turned out in their thousands to vote for the new Assembly and Executive of 2007, and who put it into the hands of Paisley and McGuinness. When you watch now, it is almost possible to forget the war, the years of killing, the political stalemates and stand-offs, the hopelessness. Now, there is a confidence that the war is over, that dissident republicans cannot destabilise the new order, that this deal, for all its strangeness and peculiarity and the fact that it was once unthinkable, can be made work, and will be made to work.

Loyalist paramilitary brigadier Jackie McDonald, speaking at a UDA Remembrance Sunday event in November 2007, acknowledged both the incredulity and the inevitability of the final deal:

> I agree with what Ian Paisley is doing. He has to do it. I know a lot of people are not happy. He has to make progress. We have to have an Assembly. We have to have devolved government. Whatever the price, we have to have it. We have to move on.
>
> I supported him when he did it [entered government with Sinn Féin]. I hoped he would do it before he did it, and I still support him. I still agree with what he is doing.

McDonald understands the political decision-making that guided Paisley in 2007, but he also remembers the past and is concerned that the loyalist community will become the forgotten people of the peace process.

> When he [Paisley] said he despised loyalist paramilitaries, I just had to shake my head. Look at where he is sitting now and where we have come from, and what our people have done on behalf of people making blood and thunder speeches. And I think of Martin McGuinness, and I suppose in some other sort of way his community would have the same reservations about what he has done [entering government with Paisley], but he [McGuinness] wouldn't give the UDA 2d. He has given us all 3d—death, he has given us destruction and he has given us despair.

This is what lies just beneath the surface. Yes, McDonald wants the new political arrangement to work, even though he knows it contradicts so much of what was said and done in the past. The steps Paisley took in those spring months of 2007 were the biggest in his political career—moments of real leadership.

He helped make the new government and that in turn helped cement the peace. A year later, our politics have moved beyond the Paisleys. Peter Robinson replaced the ageing Paisley as First Minister and DUP leader; Jeffrey Donaldson moved into the Stormont Executive. They will know there is unfinished business both in the political and the peace processes. Despite what Martin McGuinness said earlier, there are those in the DUP who are still looking over their shoulders at Jim Allister, and there are senior party figures clearly uncomfortable in this new Stormont arrangement with republicans. This is making progress difficult to achieve on a number of political issues. On another issue, this time in the peace process, further progress is also needed. The loyalists still have their guns, and while no one should be left in the trenches, loyalism needs to demonstrate a credible end to all its wars.

Chapter 7

The Union remains safe

*If as it seems that we are coming to the endgame
now—that the war is over, we have to make sure that
when we call it, we call it right, and that anything that
we say in any declaration now or in the future will
basically be upheld. We have never been in the business
of a quick fix just for the optics. There's no point saying
that an organisation is preparing to leave the stage
when, in fact, on the ground, it is not. So, basically the
consultation period has been so long simply because we
want to make sure when we call it, it is called right and
people can have confidence in what we say. We certainly
do believe that there was a sizeable act of [IRA] decommissioning—but we do realise that they still retain a
sizeable arsenal ... We believe that the Provo war is
finished. We believe that now it has turned to unarmed
struggle ... We don't believe there is a will on their
behalf to go back to war. There certainly remains a
capability. That is beyond doubt. Our threat assessment
is there is not the will nor the inclination.*
(UVF LEADERS IN TAPED INTERVIEW WITH AUTHOR,
30 AUGUST 2006.)

*They say a pike in the thatch and all the rest of it.
But I believe that it's a comfort factor for them. Now,
I look forward, if I am still living, to stand on some
podium to say that the UVF have decommissioned*

*their weapons. That would be my dream—that would
be, I suppose, maybe the icing on the cake.*
(GUSTY SPENCE ON HIS HOPES FOR UVF
DECOMMISSIONING.)

*The Ulster Defence Association believes that the war is
over and we are now in a new democratic dispensation
that will lead to permanent political stability … The
Ulster Defence Association is committed to achieving a
society where violence and weaponry are ghosts of the
past … all active service units of the [UDA-linked] Ulster
Freedom Fighters will as of 12pm tonight stand down
with all military intelligence destroyed, and as a consequence of this all weaponry will be put beyond use.*
(UDA LEADERSHIP STATEMENT, REMEMBRANCE
SUNDAY, 11 NOVEMBER 2007.)

November 1993: I did not know him then, but this date
marked the first time I met David Ervine. The meeting
took place in a building on the Shankill Road, a building of narrow passages and considerable security, a heavy door
at the front, a metal gate inside. This was before the ceasefires
of 1994; it was wartime. The man who met me wore a cap, had
a distinctive voice and a thick, dark moustache. He did not
introduce himself by name, but soon he would emerge from
that loyalist building and background onto the public stage.

This is the first time I have written about David Ervine's
involvement in that meeting back in November 1993. It was a
friendly greeting. We went upstairs into a room where two other
men were waiting. I had met one of them before and knew the
other because of who he was—a man of the highest rank in the
UVF and someone I now believe has been a long-time Special
Branch informer. This, I believe, was the first time we chatted, if

you could call it that. He told me there was no need for intro-
ductions. The man who was with him was, and still is, part of
the UVF's 'Command Staff'. Ervine stayed in the room for the
duration of the meeting and then showed me out. A plot by the
UVF to smuggle a huge arms shipment into Northern Ireland
had just been foiled and the weapons and explosives intercept-
ed at Teesport, in England. There was an envelope on the table
in that meeting room and inside it a statement from the loyalist paramilitary organisation. I was asked to remove it and read
it, and it was kind of what I expected.

The capture of the arms shipment was described as 'a logisti-
cal setback' and the UVF stated that 'it in no way diminishes our
ability nor our determination to carry on the war against the
IRA'. There was a message from the paramilitary leadership to
the loyalist people, and an appeal for support:

> We would ask them in these dark days to continue that sup-
> port in the sure and certain knowledge that we will remain
> unbowed and unbroken.

The loyalists of the UVF and the Shankill feared being sold out
by the British. A peace project was being developed by the
leader of the Republican movement, Gerry Adams, and the
leader of the Social Democratic and Labour Party, John Hume;
Dublin was also involved. It spooked the loyalists and prompted
all of that talk of dark days and continuing war. Yet the UVF men
in that room in November 1993 were the makers of a loyalist
ceasefire declared just eleven months later and, to this day, they
hold the most senior paramilitary positions. David Ervine is
dead. One of the creators of our peace did not live long enough
to see the political era of Paisley and McGuinness, although he
believed and predicted it would happen.

Ervine grew out of that UVF organisation and background
into the peace process, but he never denied his roots. I was at his

bedside when he died, invited there by his wife, Jeanette. We had become very good friends—friends from different sides of the religious fence, and although a journalist and a politician, we could be comfortable in each other's company, knowing we could say and said what was on our minds, no matter how difficult. Loyalism has been sullied by some of those who were given a rank and a role, such as John Gregg, Johnny Adair, Jim Gray, John White and the Shoukri brothers, among others. Ervine lifted loyalism to the level of political respectability. He did so because when he spoke about peace, he meant it. His war ended a very long time ago. In May 2007 Prime Minister Tony Blair put his name to these words:

> David Ervine was a proud son of Ulster who grew up in a particular place, at a particular time, but who learned that the best way to defend and promote his tradition was to talk, not fight. It was for his fluency and his ability in doing that, that he was respected and admired by all sides in the Northern Ireland peace process.

In January 2007 we all saw what Tony Blair meant—in the remarkable occasion of David Ervine's funeral. He was fifty-three years old when he died, his life cut short by a heart attack and stroke. He was alive and well when we chatted late on Saturday, 6 January. Hours later he was in hospital; by Monday he was dead. What I witnessed, and what many others saw, in the days that followed his passing was a confirmation that our war was indeed over. It was something very real that you could see and feel, and it was crystallised in one memorable moment: Gerry Adams, the man on the other side of the war, the republican who was the enemy, came to the church in the heart of loyalist east Belfast for the celebration of David Ervine's life. Alex Maskey, a former Sinn Féin Lord Mayor of Belfast, accompanied Adams. They were welcomed by David's brother, Brian, and applauded in the church. It was quite something—hard to put into the right words, but a moment that spoke for itself and that spoke loudly of a changing place that was beginning to discover peace. Under its roof, inside that church, all sorts of people were knit together in a moment that was both joyful and sad.

The leadership figures of the UVF were there, too, as was Jackie McDonald, the most prominent of the UDA's brigadiers. They sat in the same church as the Chief Constable Sir Hugh Orde and the Northern Ireland Secretary of State Peter Hain, in a congregation that included Gerry Adams, the former Irish Taoiseach Albert Reynolds and Irish Foreign Minister Dermot Ahern. Something smaller, but still significant, had happened forty-eight hours before the funeral. Two of Adams' party colleagues, Jim Gibney and Tom Hartley, visited the Ervine home, driven there by my wife, Val. She took them on a nervous journey down the loyalist Albertbridge and Newtownards roads, up into the Braniel estate and to the door of the Ervine home. I was inside. While they were there, many loyalists arrived at the house—paramilitary, political and community loyalists. I watched with my own eyes what was happening. These were not publicity stunts. This was about respect. And in all of this there was a considerable risk. On Adams' attendance at the funeral, a senior UVF leader commented: 'There's nobody saying that shouldn't have happened, and most people, privately if not openly, appreciated that it happened—that he [Adams] had the balls to be there.' It was significant that Adams was there, but also significant that the UVF let it happen.

The weeks that followed delivered a new power-sharing government to Northern Ireland. Loyalists kept their place in the political mainstream when Dawn Purvis retained David Ervine's Assembly seat in east Belfast, and the leadership of the UVF made its contribution to this new beginning. In its own words it told us that its part in the loyalist war was now over.

This fighting organisation would 'assume a non military, civilianised role'. Recruitment, military training and targeting had ceased and all intelligence information was 'rendered obsolete'. The organisation had 'deactivated' its active service units and its 'ordnance' [weapons] had been 'put beyond reach'—although not beyond use. This had been delivered by the two men I met in that room in November 1993, when their statement was set in a context of 'dark days'. Now, they were telling us that the war was over.

Belfast, 3 May 2007: this was a day that was a long time coming, and it came too late for David Ervine. It was the UVF's day, the day on which that organisation returned to the scene of the original loyalist ceasefire of 1994. It took us back to Fernhill House, not far from the main Shankill Road in Belfast. Inside was a podium draped with a Union flag; the microphones and cameras were waiting for Gusty Spence. Thirteen years had passed since he read the words of the Combined Loyalist Military Command ceasefire. Now, there was another statement for him to deliver, and it was being presented as the UVF's endgame, just days before Paisley and McGuinness were set to become First and Deputy First Ministers. The timing of the statement therefore had more than a little significance. As the new political era was about to open up, these particular loyalists wanted to say that their part in the war was over. Yet for all the UVF said that day, so much was left unsaid.

Ervine was much like Spence—able to think for himself and to think differently, able to talk for himself and to talk differently. As a result, he stood out in his community. Loyalism misses him; the peace process misses him; Spence describes him as 'irreplaceable'. He was certainly missed on that May day when the endgame statement was being presented. There were things that needed to be said that were not said, things that needed explanation that were not explained. I imagine he would have said and done it differently, but unfortunately it came too late. This latest statement was the result of months and months and months of talking inside two organisations, the UVF and the associated Red Hand Commando. Spence had a significant input into the 1994 ceasefire declaration, but not this statement of May 2007. It was written in a way that made for awkward reading; even Spence struggled with it. It was also delivered only once it was safe to do so. There was no risk anymore. The IRA was gone and the new politics settled in this arrangement between the DUP and Sinn Féin. It would have meant more had it been delivered earlier and if more had been said and done. In its endgame, the UVF simply put its guns 'beyond reach', but not beyond use.

'It [that decision] eradicates the rest of the statement,' Spence told me in an interview for this book. Remember who it was speaking these words—the man who, somewhat reluctantly, agreed to read this latest statement on behalf of the UVF. This is its text:

ULSTER VOLUNTEER FORCE & RED HAND COMMANDO COMMAND STAFF, BELFAST, THURSDAY 3 MAY 2007

Following a direct engagement with all units and departments of our organisation, the leadership of the Ulster Volunteer Force and Red Hand Commando today make public the outcome of our three year consultation process. We do so against a backdrop of increasing community acceptance that the mainstream Republican offensive has ended; that the six principles upon which our ceasefire was predicated are maintained; that the principle of consent has been firmly established and thus, that the Union remains safe. We welcome recent developments in securing stable, durable democratic structures in Northern Ireland and accept as significant support by the mainstream Republican Movement of the constitutional status quo.

Commensurate with these developments, as of twelve midnight, Thursday 3 May 2007, the Ulster Volunteer Force and Red Hand Commando will assume a non-military, civil-ianised, role.

To consolidate this fundamental change in outlook we have addressed the methodology of transformation from a military to civilian organisation by implementing the following measures in every operational and command area:

All recruitment has ceased.

Military training has ceased.

Targeting has ceased and all intelligence rendered obsolete.

All Active Service Units have been deactivated.

All ordnance [weapons] has been put beyond reach and the Independent International Commission on Decommissioning [IICD] instructed accordingly.

We encourage our volunteers to embrace the challenges which continue to face their communities and support their continued participation in non-military capacities. We reaffirm our opposition to all criminality and instruct our volunteers to cooperate fully with the lawful authorities in all possible instances. Moreover, we state unequivocally, that any volunteer engaged in criminality does so in direct contravention of Brigade Command and thus we welcome any recourse through due process of law. All volunteers are further encouraged to show support for credible restorative justice projects so that they, with their respective communities, may help eradicate criminality and anti-social behaviour in our society.

We ask the government to facilitate this process and remove the obstacles which currently prevent our volunteers and their families from assuming full and meaningful citizenship.

We call on all violent dissidents to desist immediately and urge all relevant governments and their security apparatus to deal swiftly and efficiently with this threat. Failure to do so will inevitably provoke another generation of loyalists towards armed resistance.

We have taken the above measures in an earnest attempt to augment the return of accountable democracy to the people of Northern Ireland and as such, to engender confidence that the constitutional question has now been firmly settled.

In doing so we reaffirm the legitimacy of our tactical response to violent nationalism yet reiterate the sincere expression of abject and true remorse to all innocent victims of the conflict.

Brigade Command salutes the dedication and fortitude of our Officers, NCOs and Volunteers throughout the difficult, brutal years of armed resistance. We reflect with honour on those from our organisation who made the ultimate sacrifice, those who endured long years of incarceration and the loyal families who shared their suffering and supported them throughout.

Finally we convey our appreciation for the honest forth-right exchange with Officers, NCOs and Volunteers through-out the organisation over the past three years which has allowed us to assume with confidence the position we adopt today.

For God and Ulster

Captain William Johnston; Adjutant.

ENDS

Captain William Johnston is to the UVF what P. O'Neill is to the IRA—the name it uses to sign its leadership statements. In its words, you can read what I mean about this being safe. The UVF was accepting that the IRA's war was over and that the political and constitutional issues of Northern Ireland had been settled. It waited until the very last minute to do this, waited for others to do the heavy lifting—the IRA ending its armed campaign,

decommissioning and accepting policing; Paisley stepping
forward into a political arrangement with republicans and
McGuinness. The one issue that did involve risk was avoided,
and this is where I think the statement showed a lack of leadership. Remember, this is the organisation that perpetrated the
Dublin-Monaghan bombs, the Loughinisland pub shooting
and many other sectarian attacks and killings. Its guns and
bombs were a significant part of the conflict, but in this
endgame statement the UVF described its part in that war as
legitimate. The IRA, in the company of witnesses, set a standard
on the arms question that the loyalists failed, and continue to
fail, to match. Look at what they said in this statement: 'all
ordnance has been put beyond reach and the IICD instructed
accordingly'. Those weapons are not beyond the reach of the
UVF organisation. For all its other significant and important
words on 3 May, the organisation did not meet the requirements of the decommissioning process. The IICD made that
absolutely clear in a statement issued on the same morning as
the UVF statement:

> We are concerned by their intention to deal with their arms
> without the involvement of the IICD. Without the
> Commission's involvement, action on arms does not meet
> the requirements of the decommissioning legislation nor the
> agreement reached by the parties in the Belfast Agreement.
> We are ready to meet with the UVF to discuss how we can
> work together to deal with their arms.

Forty-eight hours earlier, on the Shankill Road, I had met the
UVF leadership—three of its Brigade Command and a fourth
man, whom I believe was the author of a significant part of the
statement as well as being one of the key organisers of the
Spence news event. The meeting would be best described, I
suppose, as bad-tempered; several times I thought about getting

up and leaving. It was angry and confrontational. At times, it was insulting. Of the four I met, one did most of the talking—the man of the most senior rank in the UVF. He is one of those whom I quote at the opening of this chapter. Our talking goes back many years, back into that meeting I described on the Shankill Road in 1993, when the UVF had lost its arms shipment at Teesport. Fourteen long years later, on 1 May 2007, our conversation was again about guns, about my reporting of the now imminent UVF initiative and my focus on the question of arms. I was accused of 'raising the bar' for the UVF, was told that this statement was about 'ending conflict', that it was about 'people's lives' and not about me. As the meeting progressed, I became 'that c**t Rowan'. I was told this was how volunteers in the UVF saw me. It was obvious that my writing had caused some offence.

In their blind rage, the loyalists were missing the point. Their guns had taken many lives. Only very occasionally was their war a confrontation with republicans. More often than not their victims were 'non-combatants'—innocent, uninvolved Catholics who were killed because of their religion. And those guns that had spilled so much blood were being kept—albeit 'beyond reach', whatever that actually meant. That is something that has not been explained, not then and not since. The UVF was missing the point and as a result was about to miss the moment. Just a week down the road, on 8 May, the reign of Paisley and McGuinness would commence. The UVF had an opportunity to give so much more to this occasion, participate fully in it, but instead it chose to keep its guns, to play it safe and thereby to come up short in its words and its deeds.

I want to set out here one of the offending articles I wrote, published in the *Belfast Telegraph* on Friday 20 April 2007 under the headline: 'UVF set for arms deal—but where's the cache?'

It was a pointed comment and it was said for a purpose. The senior security source who spoke to this newspaper earlier this week wanted the UVF to hear what he was saying—hear it before that organisation issues its statement on "future intent". That statement—expected very soon—has been in the making for a number of years, the endpoint of a long internal consultation process inside the UVF and associated Red Hand Commando. And inside the intelligence world they have a pretty good idea about what's going to be said. They've had a long time to put their jigsaw together, and they know what the loyalists are thinking about doing and not doing with their weapons. That's what brought the very specific comment from that senior security source when he spoke to this newspaper a few days ago. "People who think that they can have a private army and weapons—bunkered or not—[need to know] it's not a runner." In that sentence that source revealed the loyalist plan. There will be no decommissioning. Instead, the loyalists will use words to explain that their weapons have been put away by them and by their quartermasters never to be used again. But who will believe them? More than a hundred people have just been warned that their details have been found in the hands of the loyalist organisation. And, yes, when it speaks, the UVF may well tell us that all intelligence information it has gathered over the years is now "obsolete", and, yes, that will be an important statement. But its decision on its weapons has all the potential to make small a statement of considerable significance. How can you end your war and keep your guns? The UVF started talking to itself about all of this before the IRA decisions of 2005—the initiative that ended the armed campaign and led to the decommissioning seen by the witnesses Alec Reid and Harold Good. That putting beyond use of IRA weapons happened at nine different locations. And all of that has set a new standard. The UVF has had two years to adjust its thinking—to do what the IRA did, to do something that will fit into the new circumstances and the new political era of Ian Paisley and Martin McGuinness. As that security source commented earlier this week, "May 8 changes everything". The loyalist paramilitary leadership is about to change the UVF and Red Hand Commando—order an end to many of its activities, but in clinging to its weapons, it is making a huge mistake. To quote a senior political source, it is leaving its statement open to "ridicule". Will any of that matter to the UVF? Is it likely to change anything at this late stage? The loyalists are going to put their own guns away. They know what others will think and say about all of that. But there is a "so be it" kind of attitude. We should be able to read the small print very soon, and it will be then that a judgement will be made on the worth of this loyalist initiative. That's when people will decide if this part of the loyalist war is really over.

You can see from this article just how much was known about what the UVF was going to say. There was no intrigue, and on the arms issue it had that unmissable flaw running right through it. By highlighting this, I was making things difficult for the UVF, meddling in something that was none of my business. That was the thrust of the argument in that meeting on 1 May. The man who did most of the talking that day gives orders and is used to being obeyed, but I am not one of his soldiers, and my job is different from his. That was my counter-argument. As often happens to a journalist in a conflict situation, I was in a no-win situation. There are always those who want journalists to become part of the process. Those people try to pressure you into doing things their way. That was what that confrontation was all about: the UVF feared that its statement would be dismissed in a negative media response, and they were trying to change the tone of the coverage.

I wrote about that meeting a few days later and made public the argument over this issue of guns. Then, the following month, I wrote the following article for the *Belfast Telegraph* under the headline: 'What does 'beyond reach' really mean?'

To ask the question is to be awkward, unhelpful—to say out loud what people don't want to hear. What does "beyond reach" mean in the context of the weapons of the UVF and the Red Hand Commando, and why ask the question again? There are good reasons for doing so. After its endgame statement of 3 May consideration is now being given to "de-specifying" the UVF. It means its ceasefire would again be recognised after that status was lost in all the madness of events linked to the Whiterock Orange march in 2005, and in the UVF-LVF feud of that same period. Just before the UVF announcement of last month—two days before it to be precise—Secretary of State Peter Hain met a loyalist political and paramilitary delegation. That delegation was told that the UVF could be de-specified depending on the detail of the then imminent loyalist statement. Does the Northern Ireland Office now have the answers to allow it to make its judgement? Does it know—does anyone know—what "beyond reach" means? I remember the period of the Castlereagh robbery, the republican arrests in Colombia and the Stormontgate scandal. Sinn Féin didn't like or want a focus on those events. To suggest IRA involvement as part of a journalistic assessment of information was to be anti-peace process, to be awkward, to be unhelpful, and as a consequence was to be shunned by some republicans. Now, to ask questions about loyalist weapons is to "raise the bar" for the UVF. So, you are expected to pretend with others that the question of these guns has been dealt with. It has not. General John de Chastelain and his Commission [the IICD] have been clear on that. Their response to the UVF-Red Hand Commando statement of 3 May, when they explained that the loyalists had not met the requirements of the decommissioning legislation, was dismissed in the words "too bad". Would

the IRA have got away with that? We all know the answer to
that question. There is something not right about the decision
earlier this week to wash away any prospect of security force
charges in relation to the Pat Finucane murder and other
cases. And there is something not right about the political attitude when it comes to loyalist guns. That is why de Chastelain
can be dismissed with the words "too bad". "Beyond reach"
means nothing. Those guns, if the UVF and Red Hand
Commando need them, are still within their reach. Is that
something that should be considered as the status of the UVF is
reviewed? Of course it is, but will it? That loyalist paramilitary
statement of last month was significant in what it said about
ending targeting and recruitment, what it said about active
service units being de-activated and intelligence information
now being obsolete. All of that makes a contribution to the
peace process, and Peter Hain—or whoever makes the final
decision on the UVF's ceasefire—would be right to acknowledge
that. They would be wrong to ignore the unfinished business
that is the issue of loyalist guns. That question isn't going to
go away—nor should it. Nor—despite the announcement
earlier this week—will the issue of security force collusion in
the Finucane and other killings. And there is a bigger scandal.
It has to do with those in loyalist leadership who were, and
maybe still are, in the pay of the Special Branch and the
Security Services. It goes to the top of the UDA and the UVF, to
men at the decision-making heart of those organisations—
men who directed the terror campaigns of those groups. They
think they are a protected species—that they are untouchable.
Is that why they get away with the nonsense of weapons
beyond reach? There is a double standard, and to ask the
question is not to be awkward, not to be unhelpful, not to be
anti-peace process, but to ask it because it needs asking—
asked, not just for people living outside the loyalist communities, but for those who live within them.

(The UVF was de-specified in May 2008. There had still been no decommissioning.)

In this process loyalist guns are politically unimportant and therefore were never part of the deal-making at the highest political level. Accordingly, there was never the same focus or the same demands when it came to the UDA, the Red Hand Commando and the UVF decommissioning their weapons. That lack of focus represents a political double standard. Read the words of the UVF leaders at the opening of this chapter, their acceptance that the 'Provo war is finished' and their assessment that there is neither 'the will nor inclination' to resume an armed campaign. Then read its statement of 3 May 2007 and its view that the political and constitutional questions of Northern Ireland have been settled. The only concern the UVF had in the build-up to its declaration was the prospect of a joint British–Irish Government Plan B should Sinn Féin and the DUP fail to make a deal. That fear disappeared in the arrangements that heralded the era of Paisley and McGuinness, yet the UVF still kept its guns. No IRA threat, no political or constitutional threat, no Dublin threat—all said out of the mouth of the UVF, but no decommissioning and no pressure to do so because, politically, it doesn't matter.

One man knew the loyalists were making a mistake—Gusty Spence:

I said, why not take the ultimate step? It wouldn't only add to the statement. It would make the statement. The weapons are finished.

This is Spence recalling a conversation in his home with three men, including the UVF leader, in the days leading up to the statement. He describes that meeting as 'hammer and tongs—hot and heavy':

They said a thing in the statement. It even galled me to read it out, but I read it out anyhow, that the arms had been bunkered—beyond reach—and the General [de Chastelain] had been contacted. I told them, I said, that means nothing.

Why, then, did he read it? Spence has a ready answer—because he did not want to 'stymie the announcement'. However, he agrees that decommissioning will be achieved only if there is leadership direction:

> If you are the leader, you lead from the front—perhaps maybe after consultation—you have to have the confidence in yourself, the confidence in your men [to say], 'I'm making a direct order here that UVF arms will be dispensed with—decommissioned, call it what you want. I expect every man to obey that.'

The confidence to give that order was not there, which in turn embedded in the UVF's statement a very visible flaw. The bigger flaw, however, was in the process that allowed this to happen, that made the loyalist guns less important. The loyalists saw themselves as being on the same side as the British and the security forces, on the one side fighting against the IRA, yet still they dismiss any suggestion of a cosy relationship, as a senior UVF figure made clear to me:

> Their theory [the republican theory] has always been that a UVF man couldn't have mounted any operation unless there was a Special Branch man driving the car or an MI5 officer passing material. So, it fits in nicely with their agenda. The reality of things, and the IRA needs to realise this, the reality was Ulstermen fighting the IRA, on their own with what bits and scraps of information that they could gather ... For to suggest, as some people do, that basically the loyalist organisations as a whole were driven by the security forces or

Special Branch or MI5, it beggars belief. I mean the war would
have been over a long time ago.

This is what you would expect to hear from the man who spoke
those words—the most senior figure in the UVF leadership—
but there is now simply too much proof of collusion, too much
information pointing to the most senior loyalists operating in
agent roles for that refrain to be acceptable. The loyalists have
always been treated differently in the peace process. They have
never been subjected to the same weight of focus with regard to
their actions and their guns. The UDA, for all its killing, did not
become a proscribed organisation until 1992—when the first of
the ceasefires was almost upon us. And the biggest scandal is the
story of the loyalist agents, which I touched upon in that article
in the *Belfast Telegraph* in June 2007. This, I think, takes us into
the murkiest areas of the war, into places that were never meant
to be exposed. It also takes us to the very top of the UDA and UVF
organisations, into the leaderships that were directing the loyalist war. This is at the level of the Brigade Command and the
Inner Council. It can go no higher. I know who these men are—
their names, their positions, and their roles not just within
loyalism but with the Special Branch. What was this war?

Several times I have seriously considered naming the agents,
but then I thought about their lives, and my life. To know them
and not to name them was, I felt, to collude in some way in what
had happened, to be part of the cover-up, part of the silence.
When you become involved in these things as a journalist
because of the information you hold, you are caught between
the rock and the hard place, between life and death. The more
I study loyalism and the more I find out about it, the more
questioning I become. What is it now in our peace? What was it
in the war? Yes, it can be argued that the agents helped direct a
movement towards peace, but they were also part of the killing
process. They were part of both—the killing and the ending of

the killing. Is that what happens in conflict? Is it the norm, something we just have to accept? There is another question: when you are running agents at the level of the Command Staff and Inner Council, how close are you to actually directing and controlling those organisations? It is clear that these things were nowhere as simple as the UVF leader has suggested, nowhere near as simple as gathering up bits and scraps of information. Far from it. That UVF leader is the suspected long-time agent—another informer is one of the UDA's Belfast brigadiers.

The killing of the Belfast solicitor Pat Finucane alone raises so many questions because so many agents were involved with the Army and the Special Branch before, during and after that shooting: Tommy Lyttle, who was the UDA 'brigadier' on the Shankill Road at the time; William Stobie, a paramilitary quartermaster; Brian Nelson, who was working as an army agent and collating UDA intelligence; Ken Barrett, possibly the driver for the gunmen and recruited by the Special Branch after the shooting, as was one of his closest associates in the UDA in west Belfast—a man who still holds a significant paramilitary rank. One killing, so many questions, but the answers continue to evade us. I did name one of the loyalist agents publicly in a report for the *Belfast Telegraph* published in February 2006. I named John White because he had already fled Northern Ireland; I named him as an example of what was accepted practice in what we called the *dirty war*. White was a drug dealer and convicted murderer who, after his release from jail, became closely linked with Johnny Adair; that was an open secret in the loyalist community. Yet he could still be in the pay of the Special Branch. White was an agent as close to Adair as anyone could be, and Adair made loyalism rotten. Men like Adair and White are the reason why loyalism struggles for respectability and credibility. In the public mind, the loyalist leadership has not been able to create sufficient distance between the various organisations and those individuals.

The loyalist world is a complicated place of competing organisations, competing leaderships and competing interests. It is
also a place that is plagued by paranoia and self-doubt. I am not
sure that they have been able to come to terms with the peace
process, with the ending of the 'Provo war', as they describe it,
and all that that means. That UVF statement of May 2007 asserts
and insists that the Union is still safe. Is it themselves they are
trying to persuade in that statement? There are those in their
community who still believe that Ulster is being sold out, who
fear Martin McGuinness in government and the north–south
dimension to Northern Ireland's politics. The loyalist world is a
place of contradictions—confused, fragmented, broken up into
many different pieces and fearing itself as much as anything
else. This is where you will find the real story behind that flawed
decision to keep the guns. They want to protect themselves
from each other and from something that has been allowed to
grow up under the loyalist leadership.

I am not sure that the Command Staff and the Inner Council
are in control of the loyalist destiny, not anymore. This is suggested by what is happening in the ranks below them and across
their communities. Those who have the money, the drugs and
the guns own the influence within those organisations, and it
may be too late to suppress that growing culture of gangsterism
and criminality. And yet, go back just a decade or so and you
will find leadership decisions that were informed and forward-
thinking. There was, for example, no knee-jerk response to the
IRA bomb in Canary Wharf in 1996 and no reaction to the
Omagh bomb of 1998. Those who had rank in the Command
Staff of the UVF and Red Hand Commando and in the Inner
Council of the UDA held their people and their organisations
back. They did so at a time when it would have been easier—
more popular in terms of the loyalist mood—to let them go, but
the leaderships made a different, more difficult, choice. That
was important and valuable in preserving at least some of the

peace back then. Unfortunately, as the process has developed, that quality of leadership has been lost, even though many of the same people are still in place. Loyalism does not have a McGuinness or an Adams or any identifiable leaders of that kind and it does not have the cohesiveness of the Republican Movement. It is a very different kind of animal.

Loyalism, as I have said, is a loose collection of organisations, leaderships, groups of people and individuals. They are not sure about each other. Many fear their own ghosts. They are struggling with an enemy within their own ranks. The contradiction inherent in loyalism is easily illustrated by looking at two influential individuals: Johnny Adair and David Ervine. Adair is a gangster; Ervine was what I would call a 'cause' loyalist. He was the closest thing they had to an Adams or a McGuinness, but he never had those men's authority or position of leadership. He was not a part of the UVF Brigade Command, and those who wanted to travel at a slower pace within the peace process held him back. Inside loyalism there was jealousy and suspicion of Ervine because he was different. He understood the peace process and what had to be done, but, at times, just could not persuade the paramilitary leadership to do it.

The crux of the problem for loyalism today is that it still has not separated, in a public, credible, convincing way, the Ervines from the Adairs, and of course I mean that in a much wider sense than those two individuals. The paramilitary leadership tolerates the gangsters. That tolerance and that presence are destroying loyalism, and the weakness thus inculcated is destroying their communities. Loyalism has become the ugly blot on the landscape of peace. That is how it is viewed. That is why those who are trying to do the right thing need to separate themselves from those who have spent their lives preying on their own community. Many have used the cover and the name of loyalism to build a dictatorship that has terrorised their own people. That is why, when it comes to elections, there are so few votes for loyalist candidates. The privacy of the polling station has been the people's revenge, because it affords them the only way of fighting and answering back.

Look at the trends within that loyalist paramilitary world since the original ceasefire of 1994, which was declared in the name of the Combined Loyalist Military Command, at a time when there was a respected political leadership within that community. Look at the feuds: between the UVF and the LVF, between the UDA and the UVF, between the UDA and the LVF, and within the UDA. There is the evidence of the power struggles, the fight for control, the fight for the direction and the destiny of loyalism, and there too is the reason why the loyalists keep their guns and refuse to put them beyond use. It has nothing to do with the IRA, nothing to do with the Provo war, nothing to do with the dissident republican threat, nothing to do with the new politics, nothing to do with any constitutional arguments, nothing to do with what the loyalists claim their fight was about. No, it is about themselves, about the fear with which they regard each other, about not being able to trust each other and, for those reasons, about not being able to deliver—being unable to match what the IRA did in September 2005 in a decommissioning process involving an international commission and Church witnesses.

Today, and for the foreseeable future, the loyalist war is within. It is a struggle between the 'cause' loyalists and the 'criminal' loyalists, but in its tolerance of that criminality across its communities, the paramilitary leaderships risk surrendering their authority to those in the lower ranks. In their decision-making, those leaderships are already being dictated to and directed by those below, and they are losing control. They are making and measuring their orders to fit a mood, not having the confidence to give instructions shaped by their own thinking and expect them to be obeyed. The leadership that was so evident, and that saved some of the peace in those dark days of 1996 and 1998, is being eroded and lost.

The biggest muddle and structural mess is the UDA organisation, if one can even call it such. Here, there are so many wheels within wheels, a clatter of cooks spoiling the broth. There is an Inner Council of brigadiers. Adair held that rank, as did Andre Shoukri and Jim Gray—one of them in exile, one of them in jail, the other dead, and all of them in the category of 'criminal' loyalist. Their climb into positions of leadership shows the pattern: they have been forced out now, but they all got to the top. The loyalist battle is the continuous fight to curtail that trend. This is what saps its energy and stunts its community and political growth. In the public mind, loyalism has become identified and characterised in the image of the gangsters, miring it in a swamp of drug dealing, extortion and other criminal acts. It is in that swamp that its votes, its credibility and its opportunities are being swallowed up and lost, thanks to the actions of a minority. Is it too late for the majority to win out and reassert themselves? Only they can answer that question.

On its march towards its endgame, the UDA walked in hobnail boots. There is nothing discreet or tactful about this organisation. Its dirty washing always hangs in public—the feuding, the power struggles, the criminality of drugs and extortion, it's always visible, always needing to be addressed. It can be read in the statement of the UDA leadership on Remembrance Sunday 2007. It was a statement about war and politics, but it was dragged into the issue of crime, so much so, in fact, that that paramilitary leadership had to give 'a general order to all members not to be involved in criminality':

> It is the duty of every member to understand that to be involved in crime or criminality is to undermine the cause. We have had those who joined our ranks for political reasons; these men went on to give great sacrifice and brought honour to the organisation and gained the respect of their comrades. But there have been those who joined our ranks for crime

and self gain. These people must be rooted out and never be allowed to breathe in our ranks. These people have been involved in drug dealing and this must be stamped out. Drugs destroy our children and our children are our future. These people are not loyalists—they are criminals. There is no place in the organisation for such people.

This was part of the story on a day of paramilitary marching and music, of remembering and commemoration, on a day when the UDA-linked Ulster Freedom Fighters (UFF) left the stage in the furling of its flags. That was the symbolic significance of the occasion, with the UDA committing itself 'to achieving a society where violence and weaponry are ghosts of the past'. This should have been the only story that day, but the drug dealers and the criminals, as ever, stole the limelight, making it hard for those listening to believe the words, and the word, of this organisation. And so the paramilitary leadership has to speak on the issue of crime. The UDA brigadier Jackie McDonald talked that day about the organisation having to change, the need to represent the loyalist community:

… the right way—the way we used to, where we started off from, protecting our own homes, protecting our own streets, protecting our own estates.

We have to get rid of the criminality. The drug dealers must go. If you can't shoot them, shop them. Don't think anybody is an informer if they tell the PSNI where the drugs are or where the drug dealers are.

This tells us one of the reasons why the loyalists keep their guns: they fear a war with the drug dealers. McDonald said as much:

There's no place for them in the community or the organisation. They have to go. They're scum … Drug dealers have been waiting on this statement ... They may see it as some sort of weakness, or some sort of opening for them. And if they are told to go away, they could turn round and say, 'well if we don't go away, what are you going to do about it?' It is up to the community to join with the organisation, and rather than go to people's doors with baseball bats or weapons or whatever, the community is going to have to go to their doors and tell them [the drug dealers] they have to go. There is no place for them in our community.

McDonald believes a UDA without guns would be vulnerable to attack from those whose influence is growing because of their money, their drugs and their weapons. This is the new threat— the enemy within—and it is the same story right across the loyalist organisations, not just the UDA. For too long the loyalist leadership tried to hide the truth and pretend the criminality did not exist; the hiding and pretending gave rise to the problems they face today. It may be too late to win. The UDA may have already lost its authority and its influence over those who grew up in that organisation alongside Adair and Shoukri and Gray, and are now determined to do things their way.

The effect of all this can be seen running through those endgame statements released by the UVF in May 2007 and by the UDA six months later. Both organisations still have their weapons, yet both accept that the IRA war is over. When I observe loyalism, see its communities, look into the faces of its people, I wonder whether it can be rescued, whether there is the leadership and the will to try to change things. All the pandering to the loyalist organisations, all the ignoring of their activities, all of that looking away and the double standards, that failure to make decommissioning as important for them as it was on the republican side, that is what has made this mess. It is a political failure, a failure of the peace process. Just take one example: the focus there has been on the IRA's structure, even after the ending of the armed campaign, the decommissioning and the decision to support policing. In comparison, listen to what Jackie McDonald was able to say on Remembrance Sunday 2007:

> Ninety nine percent of people who we represent in the loyalist community won't hear tell of decommissioning. They're not the UDA's guns. They're the people's guns, and the people don't want to give them up.

Put that statement in the mouth of Gerry Adams—what would the reaction be? I can tell you, without any doubt, there would be no government sitting on Stormont's hill overlooking Belfast. Listen also to what Jackie McDonald said about the UDA organisation:

> The UDA is not going away. People are trying to force the UDA in a certain direction—they're damning it and demonising it every chance they get … Yes, there have been criminals within the ranks of the organisation. There have been drug dealers, but there has never been so many working hard to put that situation right, to get those people out of the organisation … The UDA should never go away. I hope it never goes away, but it has to change.

Again, put those words in the mouth of Gerry Adams, make it the IRA—what would the reaction be?

The loyalists do not need sympathy. This feeling sorry for themselves, this sense of persecution, that the world is against them, is simply part of hiding and disguising their own failings. In their statements and their speeches one can detect an inferiority complex. Somebody allowed Adair and Shoukri and Gray into places of leadership. Somebody let the criminals in—not just into the UDA but into the UVF, too—and that was tolerated for far too long. Now, loyalism has gone astray, out of the fold of the peace process. It has one political representative at Stormont, the new leader of the Progressive Unionist Party, Dawn Purvis. It is a community in which too many people do not register to vote. Why is that? Could it be because they have no faith, no trust and no time for the paramilitary leaderships? There are those in the loyalist leadership who deserve time and trust, but who have lost it because of the actions of others. In our peacetime we are watching the IRA evolve into the political process and take more prominent roles in the Sinn Féin party and in the republican community. But where are the loyalists going? What is their endpoint? What is their road, their journey?

There are those who were jealous of David Ervine, who undermined him and then cried at his funeral. Loyalism cannot afford to be jealous. It needs leadership, it needs public faces and voices and it needs those who are looking for a path back to respectability. But there are too many who have set their faces against this. The Brigade Command and the Inner Council are leaderships, but who holds the authority and the control? People have looked the other way for far too long. Now it is time to see what is happening and examine how it can be fixed. This is one of the biggest challenges still facing the peace process.

Chapter 8
End thoughts—
A table of explanation

I think international lessons would tell us on the whole the past doesn't just go away and that it stays there in some shape or form. That doesn't mean that you can't engage in different levels of forgetting to deal with that. But my personal view would be one that you can't really escape the past. And certainly when you speak with a lot of victims, they remember the past every day.
(DR BRANDON HAMBER, CHAIRMAN OF HEALING THROUGH REMEMBERING, SPEAKING TO THE AUTHOR IN SEPTEMBER 2007.)

Personal regrets, yes, of course, I have. My whole life is strewn with regrets, and I have deep, deep personal regrets ... And I had to find out what set of circumstances, historic, political or otherwise, led me to be in a cell serving a minimum of twenty years ... And whenever I went on that journey the vista was enormous, but the other journey, the journey of self questioning has to be the most hurtful journey any human being can go on—with their heart open, with their eyes open, with their brain engaged.
(FORMER UVF LEADER GUSTY SPENCE QUESTIONING WHAT HAPPENED AND HIS ROLE IN THE WAR.)

Eames and Bradley hopefully will focus on the bits of the past which currently seem to have been

*airbrushed from everyone's memory for all sorts of
reasons ... Hopefully they will come up with a consensus around how the other combatants in the past
are prepared to come to terms with what they did.
Now, I think there are all sorts of ways of doing
that ... it does range right from acknowledgment
through to amnesty. If one's really radical about it,
and I think that's where the debate needs to be, it
needs to be around the amnesty end of the business—
difficult, impossible, illegal and all that stuff ... [but]
it may start something around understanding this in
a slightly deeper way.*
(CHIEF CONSTABLE SIR HUGH ORDE ON THE
CHALLENGES AS LORD EAMES AND DENIS BRADLEY
LOOK FOR WAYS OF ANSWERING THE QUESTIONS
OF THE PAST.)

*It is impossible, I think, to recreate a context of the past
and then apply good, analytical, fair judgment ... It
is very difficult to define the context, and then I think
what you're doing is distracting people from looking
that way, looking forward, where, I think, everything
is pretty positive.*
(ARMY GOC LT GENERAL NICHOLAS PARKER
SPEAKING TO THE AUTHOR IN JULY 2007.)

How many soldiers were involved? What was it they were involved in? What were their orders? What was the objective? Even now, when it is over, many are still uncomfortable with the term 'war'. That term gives some legitimacy to the other side, the enemy in the other trenches. They called the mission Operation Banner, and it was the longest-running military operation in British Army history. Hundreds

of soldiers were killed on a battlefield of street, field, lane and
road, were killed inside their barracks, outside their barracks,
inside their homes, outside their homes. It was a bloody and
brutal series of actions and reactions stretching over decades.
The accoutrements of battle were all there: watchtowers, bases
with blast walls and high perimeter fencing, helicopters covering
foot patrols, the SAS on covert special missions. All of this had
to be dismantled into a peacetime garrison when the fighting
was finished and the mission was over. But don't call it a war.
Call it something else, anything else, don't call it what it was.

As the Army left and as Operation Banner ended, its most
senior officer in Northern Ireland, Lt General Nicholas Parker,
described the 'campaign', the 'fight', the 'challenge', the 'mission'.
Indeed, he called it everything but a war:

> The generality of what has gone on here has been that the
> Army has behaved in all its aspects impeccably, that there
> have been occasions where people have not behaved impec-
> cably, where those have been identified and proven, then
> they've been dealt with. And I think that's consistent with the
> way that we've been behaving ... The whole business of peer-
> ing back at what we've been doing, there's a real risk that you
> start to apply generalities with the benefit of hindsight, and
> you miss one of the crucial points, which is, at the time, and
> I can describe this best from my own experience. In 1974 in
> the Rodney/St James [area of west Belfast] I thought that I
> was doing the right thing, and I'm pretty certain that I was
> doing the right thing. I was behaving in what I believe was a
> reasonable fashion, but if you got a torch and [shone] it from
> now, today, on what I was doing, I think you might be
> absolutely horrified. I mean, why was I going into a house at
> four in the morning and seeing if the people that we wanted
> were there? Why was I frightened? It is impossible, I think, to
> recreate a context of the past and then apply good analytical,

fair judgment … I think it is very difficult to define the context, and then I think what you're doing is distracting people
from looking that way, looking forward, where, I think,
everything is pretty positive.

So, there is a reluctance to look back, for whatever reason, but I
agree with what the clinical psychologist Brandon Hamber said
at the top of this chapter—'the past doesn't just go away':

> One has to understand that any debate about dealing with
> the past has the risk of being swayed politically in any con-
> text, whether it is here or anywhere in the world.
>   You can hear the same debates about whose truth is going
> to be told, whose truth isn't going to be told and what issues
> are you going to look at.

Hamber is Chairman of Healing Through Remembering. He
brings international experience and learning to its debates,
including his work with witnesses to the Truth Commission in
post-apartheid South Africa:

> I think in any society there is always a deeply ambivalent view
> about whether one should look at the past. And on the whole,
> certainly when it comes to groups who have committed
> violence, they're generally fairly reluctant to go back and look
> at the past and account for their role either directly or indi-
> rectly in the past. So, I think that that's a fairly universal sense
> of reluctance about those things. That doesn't mean there
> aren't individuals, there aren't parts of those organisations …
> or that it's not possible to get to that point. But I don't see at
> this moment in time a wholesale voice coming from the
> political parties, and from the governments really commit-
> ting themselves to a deep engagement with how they are
> going to deal with the past.

Finally, the last big challenge of the peace process is to examine the truth of all that has happened. It is a process that could be as ugly as the war, which is why there are those who would prefer not to look and not to see. Different people, touched by particular events, will, of course, remember different things. They will have their own thinking and their own thoughts, and some will share them and others won't. It is going to take time and must be shaped by a process that considers not just the obvious, but everything and everyone. It is too easy to define and describe what happened in the stories of those shootings and bombings that, because of their scale, are easily recalled— the IRA and Enniskillen, La Mon and the Shankill, the loyalists in Greysteel, Loughinisland, Dublin and Monaghan. These have become our war crimes. They provide the easy answers. Yet so much else is forgotten, conveniently and otherwise. What about Bloody Sunday? What about that Army that behaved so 'impeccably'? What about those orders and those actions and those shootings in January 1972? Is this another of the war crimes? Was it killing or was it murder? Was it right or wrong? Should the truth have to be dragged out in a multi-million-pound inquiry, or is there some other way?

There is so much that begs for explanation in the story of that day and many other days—days that are considered less significant because only one person died. That is wrong. There is no point in a half-truth process or a process for propaganda purposes, concerned with victory and defeat. The talking must be about explaining and contributing to a better understanding of what happened and why. There will be people who will want to tell their stories, who will ask for nothing other than to be heard, and so there has to be someone to listen. My suggestion, as a first step in this thinking and talking process, is for a table of explanation. I set out some of my thoughts on this in an article in the *Sunday Life* newspaper on 8 July 2007:

We've now had the first meeting and the first statements, the opening words in a process that is about both the past and the future. Denis Bradley has a way with words and last week he spoke about "dealing with the shadows of the past in an acceptable and appropriate way". But who will be prepared to step out of those shadows? Bradley is co-chairing a consultative group on the past alongside the retired Church of Ireland Primate Lord Eames. And next summer they will bring forward their recommendations. I think it's time to take this particular bull by the horns. You could talk forever, consult forever, and get nowhere and go nowhere on this issue. Chief Constable Sir Hugh Orde wanted a process that asked the hard questions of all sides—including his. So let's start asking them. The talk before the consultative group was announced was that there would be "a big conversation" and a "blank sheet"—no pre-determined outcomes. In that, there is room to be bold. As part of what they are doing, the Eames/Bradley group should invite the IRA Army Council, the UVF and Red Hand Commando Brigade Staff and the UDA Inner Council to send representatives to a specially convened conference. Those who can speak for the police, the Army and the security services should also be there, as well as representatives of the relevant governments and political parties. The conference should take as long as it needs to establish what the parties to the conflict are prepared to contribute in answering and explaining that past. That's the bull by the horns. The conference is the opportunity for the questions to be put to those who have the answers. And it would allow Eames and Bradley to make a judgement on how specific, or how general, any answering of the past is going to be. There may well be arguments about "equivalence"— about the security forces in the same room as the "terrorists", but what we had was a very dirty war, not the stuff of goodies and baddies but something much more complicated and confused. And all of that is seen in the stories of [Freddie] Scappaticci and [Mark] Haddock [army and police agents inside the IRA and the UVF] and in those war games when guns were taken off and then given back to the UDA. In all that mess—and in all that messing—people died. There was a political jibe aimed at Martin McGuinness and Gerry Kelly in the Assembly last week, but this process on the past can't be about one side, can't just be about the Provos. It has to be about all sides—all of them answering and explaining, however difficult, however awkward. It is, of course, entirely possible that if such a conference were to be called, that there would be those who would stay away. Maybe more would stay away than would attend. That in itself would tell us something about who is prepared to step out of those shadows and who wants to continue to hide in them. There is an opportunity in this consultation process that Lord Eames and Denis Bradley are leading to begin to get some of the answers, or at least to begin to ask some of the questions of some of the right people. The conference, if it were to be called and attended by those invited, could be the first table of explanation—the beginnings of some breakthrough on this most delicate of all issues. We can tiptoe around it forever, or we can take the bull by the horns. Which is it to be?

Hugh Orde is one of the most radical voices on the issue of the past and how it should be addressed, why it needs to be presented in a wider frame and why it cannot just be about State killings:

Sadly we are stuck with a way forward, which is in my judgment stupid at the minute. So I think it's around how you recover that. Eames and Bradley hopefully will focus on the bits of the past which currently seem to have been airbrushed from everyone's memory for all sorts of reasons. The [focus] is clearly currently ... on State killing—period. Now, that in my view is a crazy way of dealing with the past ... That doesn't mean that you don't deal with it [the issue of State killings] ... Hopefully they [Eames and Bradley] will come up with a consensus around how the other combatants in the past are prepared to come to terms with what they did. Now, I think there are all sorts of ways of doing that. I don't think it's one-size-fits-all. I am into that spectrum ... and it does range right from acknowledgment through to amnesty. If one's really radical about it, and I think that's where the debate needs to be, it needs to be around the amnesty end of the business—difficult, impossible, illegal and all that stuff ... [but] it may start something around understanding this in a slightly deeper way. I also think some people just want to tell their story—and that helps them bring some form of closure.

The point I made about Orde earlier is again relevant here. He was not part of the war, which allows him to think more clearly and, oftentimes, more radically. He has nothing to fear in that past, is not frightened by the orders and the actions of the 1960s, 1970s, 1980s and 1990s, although he knows a lot of the story because of his role in the investigations into collusion and the Finucane murder. Nonetheless, he still wants a structured process that asks and answers the questions. He wants it because until it is done and settled, it will always be there. It is back to that point that Brandon Hamber made earlier: 'the past doesn't just go away'.

In this long process of peace-building many of the hardest questions have already been asked and answered. People had to change, organisations and parties had to change, orders and thinking and attitudes had to change. These are the things that ended the war. The lexicon of peace gave us new words to savour—dialogue, negotiation, process, compromise, healing, reconciliation, truth and justice. At times it was all painfully slow, and at times it did not work. The idea of some grand plan leading directly from A to Z is not how it worked here. After war, you make up peace as you go along. There is a momentum, a quiet confidence, that grows out of the soil of a battlefield that has been cleared. When you cannot hear the war, the overwhelming noise of its guns and bombs, you can think more clearly and you can begin to believe in change. It takes time because peace needs space in which to grow. That is something we have learned in our situation.

Someone recently was asking me in the context of another armed situation whether my message was that it was going to take them thirty years to find a way forward.

John Alderdice answered 'no' to this question and told the person asking it: 'Your situation is different.' In an interview he said to me:

We have to confess that this was a process of learning as well as a process of peace.

We came upon problems. We did not always handle them in the best way possible. We made mistakes. We had to pick ourselves up. We lost time. We didn't understand sometimes what we were doing for good and ill, and I think we've learnt a very great deal out of it. And I think there is a moral responsibility to help other people that they do not have to take so long. However, there is an issue about time. It does take a certain amount of time to work through these kinds of things.

There is a safety and a comfort in time, but there is also a danger in taking too much time. John Alderdice is right: there has to be a balance; you cannot rush peace. Look at what had to change. Look at what has changed. There is so much that this process can give to the study of conflict resolution, and there is much that it has taken from other international experiences. The process of peace-making is about helping others as much as it is about being helped by others. That is something else we have learned. Consider what was made possible as part of the ending of our very long war: the ceasefires of the IRA, the formal ending of that armed campaign, weapons put beyond use under the observation of an international commission and Church witnesses, a republican endorsement of policing and participation in political institutions. Before that happened, the process had to break through the language of 'Brits Out' and 'Not a Bullet, Not an Ounce'. Paisley was moved from the language of 'smashing' Sinn Féin to the reality of sharing power with republicans. Nobody waved a white flag. Nobody raised a victory banner. Each side gave the other the space to make peace and a political future in a process of compromises. The British Army's war footing and war presence are gone. There is now a peacetime garrison. The IRA, the RUC, the UDR, the things people fought and died for, are being allowed to fade into history.

For all that has been answered, however, there are still so many more questions to ask and more time needed to contemplate the answers. This examination and questioning of the past is a necessary part of war and peace. It is about verifying what happened, why it happened and who did what. It is the peace asking its questions of the war. At the top of this chapter Gusty Spence, one of the first men sent to jail in this fight, described his self-questioning as 'the most hurtful journey any human being can go on, with their heart open, with their eyes open and their brain engaged'. I asked did it matter to him what other people thought at the end of this decades-long war:

Not at all—couldn't care less. As Connolly said, and I'm quoting Connolly—I've no wish to be respectable in the eyes of an unrespectable world. There was a time when things hurt me, of course there was. But you see now, I'm inured to hurt. The only way you could hurt me is through my family.

I didn't ask him what he discovered on that journey of his. His description of it told me all I needed to know. The past is not going to be settled in a process of the good condemning the bad; it must be something different. This is why I am arguing for a table of explanation that, as a first step, brings all sides to the one place. Not to answer or account for what was done, but to explain from each different perspective what they think happened. What was it they thought and believed they were involved in? Why did they get involved? For that to happen, you need the 'amnesty' that Hugh Orde described earlier, however difficult that might be. The process does not have to be a picking over individual actions, more a commentary that sets a context and has the potential to offer some better understanding of events. It cannot be a story of 'no collusion', or 'I was not in the IRA', or 'we were only defending our communities'. The exploration, and the explanation, has to think beyond good and bad, has to be prepared to listen to and accept the ugly truths. There are those who will not call what we have been through a war. But how else can it be described? Think what Martin McGuinness and Sir Ronnie Flanagan could bring to a table of explanation if they could be persuaded and if the right circumstances could be created.

'The Troubles' is the label that has been attached to the decades of violence, but that name says nothing and describes nothing. Does it tell the story of the battlefield? Does it paint a picture of what it was really like? What do you see and hear in those words? It was a war and it has ended in the most unlikely of political arrangements, in something that was considered impossible for so long. Now Hugh Orde believes that those who have leadership within that new political arrangement should take responsibility and make the decisions on the past:

If people care about this place, no one can walk away from it. Now, how you can oblige those who are not part of the State to talk about the past—that's difficult … I think the only way you'll solve it [the question of the past] is you take it away from the British Government and you stick it up the hill [to Stormont]—total responsibility for dealing with it, everything, the whole thing. Until you do that, there's too many people saying, 'Not me. I'm not responsible. The British can do this'. Well, no, they can't.

As I finish this book the dissidents are still fighting, but for who and for what? They lost their war in the internal struggles within the Republican movement, in those battles within the IRA, and then when they put themselves before the people. It is over and their actions will change nothing. Blair and Ahern— no longer Prime Minister and Taoiseach—facilitated a process, gave ten years of their political lives to it, and, in the end, it answered the Irish Question. The politics are settled in that Executive now led by Peter Robinson and Martin McGuinness, which sits high on Stormont's hill and looks over a place now more at peace with itself than ever before. It is a remarkable achievement, but there is unfinished business, a final question, and that is the hardest question of all. It is the question of the past. In that past there are questions for us all—including myself—questions about what we did and what we did not do. That is why I want to end this chapter with Danny's Story— about the killing of a young man, and a question asked of me that I could not answer.

Danny McColgan is part of our past, a man whose young life was taken long after the ceasefires and the Good Friday Agreement, in a time when we thought the war was over. He was a Catholic shot dead by loyalists. Days later, on 15 January 2002, John White made a number of calls to my mobile phone.

This is John White the convicted killer, the suspected drug dealer, the close associate of Johnny Adair, and a man I was told became a covert human intelligence source—an informer in the pay of the Special Branch. It is one of those things that has made me re-think our war, what it was about and who was fighting whom. Things that once seemed straightforward now appear so much more complicated and confused. Maybe war is meant to be like that. Maybe we are not meant to understand. Maybe the fog is there for a purpose. It hides a lot, and it obscures questions that cannot be answered.

White had been out of jail for quite a number of years, since before the original loyalist ceasefire of 1994. He called me twice on that Tuesday evening in January 2002. I was in Hillsborough Castle, at a reception hosted by the Secretary of State John Reid. White wanted me to travel to the Shankill Road, in Belfast, but first we would meet on the long lane leading to Fernhill House—the venue for the loyalist ceasefire announcement in 1994. It was a dark night and, once again, I was being asked to take part in the loyalist cloak-and-dagger play. I can't say I was keen to do so.

Another journalist, Ivan Little, was also at the meeting place on that dark laneway, and we were both accompanied by cameramen. In three cars, with White leading in the first, we travelled into the heart of the Shankill, to a drinking club in Heather Street. William 'Mo' Courtney was in the room; he is a suspect in the murder of the Belfast solicitor Pat Finucane. In the drinking club on that night in January 2002, it was Courtney who ordered men in balaclavas into the room. One of them wore glasses with his mask; it was he who would read the statement.

Nothing is ever simple with the loyalists: this night, this show, was no different. At first we were told we should not record sound. When it was explained that that would mean the statement would not be heard, there was a re-think. This was happening just three days after the murder of young McColgan,

a postman shot on the sprawling Rathcoole estate on the northern outskirts of Belfast. John Gregg, one of the loyalist
brigadiers, had ordered him killed because of his religion. What
followed was a complicated sequence of statements and events.
At first, the killing was admitted in the name of the Red Hand
Defenders—a cover name used occasionally by a number of loyalist organisations. That wouldn't cut it in the new Northern
Ireland, however, the post-Agreement Northern Ireland, and the
UDA knew that a political ton of bricks was about to be dropped
on its head, so it moved to limit the damage. The UDA owned up
to the McColgan murder, but distanced itself from other threats
made against postal workers and Catholic schoolteachers.

Then the paramilitary organisation went further. It ordered
the Red Hand Defenders to stand down, set a deadline and
made threats. It was a farce. I suggested in my report that the
UDA should take a look in the mirror and repeat a hundred
times: 'I must not be a Red Hand Defender'. Courtney, I was
told, was furious (that is my word) at the dismissal of this paramilitary play. But that is all it was—a pathetic attempt to
deceive. The UDA was the Red Hand Defenders and the Red
Hand Defenders was the UDA, but in Heather Street, in all that
dressing up in paramilitary uniform and speaking from behind
masks, we were meant to believe something else.

This incident was significant for another reason. This was the
murder investigation in which the police asked for access to my
telephone records, and I had to refuse. This is the first time I
have written about this. It was not about protecting Danny
McColgan's killers; it was about protecting journalistic ethics,
my family and myself. I thought through the consequences of
saying 'yes'. How could a correspondent covering a war, living in
that war, writing about and speaking to all sides, open his
telephone record to police scrutiny? What would be the implications for personal security and for the safety of my family if I
agreed? I know the answers to those questions, but in that walk

along the thinnest of lines, I asked myself: would people under-stand if ever this became public? I have chosen to make it that.

The police were after something specific—the telephone number from which a call was made to me after Danny McColgan was shot dead. This is entirely separate from the White calls. My memory of events is that when it eventually owned up to the killing, the UDA did so using a new codeword: Cromwell. As I explained earlier in the book, these codewords are used to authenticate contacts between the paramilitary organisations and journalists. 'Cromwell' is no longer in use, which is why I have used it here. During that telephone call I was given infor-mation about the gun used to kill Danny—a weapon the UDA said had been used, if my memory serves, in two other shootings, which were also detailed. The caller, whom I knew and still know, told me he had been speaking to John Gregg. His information was detailed and clearly came from someone who knew the specifics of the McColgan killing. I told the police about the UDA statement, the admission of its involvement in the McColgan murder and what was said about the gun used. The police wanted more. They wanted to know at what time the call was made to me, and they wanted my telephone records to see if they could pinpoint the number and then the caller. I had to say no.

Some people, those who know me best and who know the job I had to do, will understand my decision; others will not. That is something I have to accept, have to live with. I knew I had no choice. John Gregg is dead now—murdered in February 2003 in a feud inside the UDA. The man in the balaclava and glasses was later jailed when expert voice-testing led to his identification. John White is in hiding. 'Mo' Courtney, at the time of writing, is in prison. I am told the man who pulled the trigger on Danny McColgan still likes to boast about what he did. I do not know his name.

The UDA made a huge mistake when it named a peace ini-tiative in memory of John Gregg. He was a war player, a man idolised because of his involvement in an ambush designed to kill Gerry Adams. It failed. Danny McColgan was one of the many innocent victims whose life cannot be given back. The information I had may have taken the police to Gregg, but not to Danny's killer. That is what I think, but perhaps that is what I want or need to believe, all these years after that question was asked of me. The question I could not answer.

A war with no winners

It looked as if there were too many people … who weren't up for this and who were out to exploit it. And one's natural human reaction was, 'Well then, fuck them. If that's it, then it's back to armed struggle'. But the head had to rule the heart, and the head knew we were in a military stalemate.
(FORMER REPUBLICAN LEADER AND IRA MEMBER DANNY MORRISON COMMENTING ON THE REACTION TO THE CEASEFIRE OF 1994.)

The realisation was the war didn't work. And the only way of moving on is to get organised and to get power … you don't have to like the people you work with. You have to engage. And I think what you saw there was that engagement.
(CHIEF CONSTABLE SIR HUGH ORDE ON THE PAISLEY–McGUINNESS GOVERNMENT AFTER THE WAR.)

The battlefield has more or less been cleared now. Only the ghosts remain. In the peace of today, they are a haunting and grim reminder of what went before—those long years of Bloody 'Everydays'. There is not one date on the calendar that is not an anniversary in the story of our dead. That is the legacy of our time in the trenches.

So what kind of war was it? In its earliest years it was something of a free-for-all, in which the British Army did what it did on the streets of Derry on Bloody Sunday and the IRA did what it did in Belfast on Bloody Friday. Both were massacres, brutal actions that have been written into the darkest days of what became known as The Troubles. It was on many occasions a war without rules, a bitter street battle in which anyone could have died. Neither the elite soldiers of the SAS or the Libyan-supplied Semtex explosive sent to the IRA changed the balance of the battle as it developed. It was a war with no winners, a stalemate in which the two principal sides fought each other to a standstill. I suppose, it could have gone on forever, but it did not. It paused, and then stopped in a realisation and acceptance of an alternative way. The fighters stepped aside and the peace process was allowed through.

I think the seeds of the endgame can be found somewhere in the 1980s, long before the ceasefires and the political process that eventually led to the historic Good Friday Agreement of April 1998 (and subsequently the St Andrews Agreement of 2006). The war was over long before it was officially declared over, but the fight continued until an acceptable way out was found, one that could not be branded surrender or victory or defeat. The British knew long before the ceasefire of 1994 that this could not and would not be ended by a military outcome. Peter Brooke, the former Conservative Northern Ireland Secretary of State, acknowledged as much in 1989 when he said that 'it was difficult to envisage a military defeat of the IRA'. In the other trenches, Adams and McGuinness also knew that the IRA could not prosecute the armed struggle to the point of a military victory. This was the deadlock out of which the peace would grow, slowly and with more killing.

Tony Blair was the British Prime Minister who made Ireland's peace possible. He allowed Adams and McGuinness into a negotiating process before the IRA disarmed. In those negotiations the battlefield was cleared, bit by bit, of IRA guns and British Army watchtowers. The two sides withdrew together, walked away from the war at the same pace. There was no white flag and no victory speeches. This was the agreed, negotiated end to all those years of fighting, and it has left Northern Ireland, or the North, more at peace with itself than ever before.

However, that honourable end, if it can be called such, was almost lost in a moment of political panic. As described earlier, behind the scenes, working through a back channel, the British were in contact with the IRA leadership in the shape of Martin McGuinness. Brendan Duddy was the link between the two sides. In the years leading to the 1994 ceasefire, the line of communication was British Government–Security Services–Duddy–McGuinness, and it operated in both directions. I think we have all misunderstood that link, believing it to have been some kind of post-box into which the Security Services and McGuinness dropped messages for Duddy to deliver. It was something more than that. In 2007 Duddy spoke to me of 'hundreds of meetings' between him and the British and 'thousands of hours of delicate dialogue—all of it aimed at creating an environment free from violence and the gun'. Duddy was never a member of the IRA. He was driven by his Christian faith: 'I completely opposed the bombs, the blood and the bullets on all sides.'

In 1993 the journalist Eamonn Mallie produced a document of proof of contacts between the British and the IRA—the same IRA that had just left its mark in the carnage of the Shankill Road bomb in Belfast. There was a Conservative Government at the time and Patrick Mayhew was the Northern Ireland Secretary of State. He claimed the contacts were linked to a message from Martin McGuinness, dated February 1993, stating that the conflict was over, but that republicans needed British advice on how to end their war. In how it was presented by Mayhew, it had more than a hint of IRA surrender. I wrote in 2007 that if McGuinness had not been McGuinness, with all his standing and credibility with the IRA leadership, he would have been finished. Remember, Northern Ireland was still at war at that time. Mayhew had thrown a hand-grenade into the nascent peace process. But Duddy is very clear:

> Martin McGuinness was psychologically not capable of asking for British advice to end the conflict—the IRA's war. That is not in Martin McGuinness' make-up or character.

McGuinness was not involved in those 'hundreds of meetings' and 'thousands of hours of delicate dialogue'. Brendan Duddy was giving his own analysis to both sides. In other words, everything that went to the British was not written or spoken or cleared by Martin McGuinness. As we look back, what is now clear is that the 'Provos' needed British help to end their war, and the 'Brits' needed McGuinness and the IRA. They needed each other to find a different way. I think that is the message that Duddy was trying to deliver through the link, not just in 1993, but over many years. And that is the analysis that became so skewed and misrepresented when Mayhew found himself in the eye of the storm in 1993. The British stood accused of talking, however indirectly, to the IRA while that organisation was still at war. That accusation engendered a political panic.

The full story of how the secret back-channel link became public has not yet emerged. However, Brendan Duddy gives us an insight into how serious it was. He told me that, at the time, he was 'interrogated' for four hours by Gerry Adams, who was determined to find out the truth behind what the British were saying. It was question after question after question, he told me. The meeting took place in Derry and Adams was accompanied by McGuinness, Gerry Kelly and Pat Doherty. They come no more senior in the republican leadership, and that leadership felt it had been 'shafted'.

One needs to understand the context of the period, to

understand the Adams–McGuinness project within republican-ism. This was 1993, and the IRA was sitting on bunkers full of Libyan weapons. It was an undefeated 'army', it was still at war, and here was this story emerging of secret contacts with the British and this claim that McGuinness—the hawk of the IRA leadership—had delivered a message that the conflict was over. Apart from a few key leadership figures, the IRA organisation would not have known of this back-channel link to the British, which is what I meant about the importance of McGuinness' credibility and standing within the IRA. Had he not been believed, he would have been dead. Duddy could have ended up dead, too. That is how dangerous things had become. It was a matter of life and death.

Just months later the IRA gave a ceasefire, but took it back in the reign of Major and Mayhew. Then it waited for Tony Blair and Bertie Ahern—the two prime ministers who steered Northern Ireland's political process towards that Good Friday Agreement. But what is the significance of the back channel? It tells us that in that long, long war, somewhere off-stage, where it could not be seen or heard, there was something going on that was about exploring an alternative to a military or security outcome.

A military analysis of the British Army's Operation Banner, written in 2006, let something out of the bag. Banner described its decades-long support role to the RUC and then the PSNI in Northern Ireland. A sentence in the document read:

The British Government's main military objective in the 1980s was the destruction of PIRA, rather than resolving the conflict.

They may not have called it a war, but the mission had a war objective, a fact raised in an interview in July 2007 with the Army's most senior soldier in Northern Ireland, Lt Gen

Nicholas Parker. I suggested to him that that sentence had the sound of war, winners and losers—victory and defeat.

'Your point is an entirely fair one,' the General accepted, on the basis of what I read to him, but then he went on to offer further explanation:

> If you look at the campaign, if I may call it a campaign. In the seventies there was a lot of action, reaction, trying to establish the carpet. The eighties, I think, was the laying of the carpet, and in that sense it is entirely legitimate that somebody says my priority at the moment is to achieve a level of security which will then allow me to shift the furniture ... But if you read it as defeat then you are slightly missing the point. That's the way they were expressing the need to provide a security environment that would let their other programmes progress.

The 'carpet' was the General's way of describing the ground upon which the politics and the peace could be built. So, I asked him, was the IRA 'destroyed' when it came to the point of ending its armed campaign in July 2005?

> I don't think that's a helpful interpretation. Because you are going back to the winning and losing, you're going back to the war. What has happened is that we have created a security environment where now the PSNI are able to do this on their own.

At the time I described the interview as a General in army boots trying to tiptoe over the eggshell that is the Northern Ireland story of the past thirty-eight years, and the military's role in that. Parker did not want to call it a war, rather it was a 'campaign', a 'mission', a 'challenge', a 'fight'. In his words, it was anything and everything but a war. Our discussion was also a military interview with an eye to the political picture, given as the Army was about to end Operation Banner and return Northern Ireland to a peacetime garrison. He was also speaking just a couple of months after the formation of the Paisley–McGuinness Executive at Stormont. I asked him about that, about McGuinness, the man of the republican enemy, now in government:

> The specific individual to me is not relevant … The point of your question, does this represent a sea change? I mean, you know it does. The fact that we have now moved where we are back with elected representatives in an Assembly who are going to be responsible for their destiny, surely that must fill us all with a sense of achievement.

This interview with this General, in that particular moment and context, was always going to leave behind many unanswered questions. That 'carpet' he spoke of was something under which much had been swept out of sight by all sides in a very dirty war. The British Government of the 1980s may well have had the military objective of destroying the IRA, but by the end of that decade it was in the back channel with the Spooks and Duddy and McGuinness, trying a different approach, looking for an alternative to victory by military means.

The full picture of Northern Ireland's peace-building is one of many pieces. John Hume, who grew up in Derry with Duddy, talked to Adams when such talking was regarded with distaste and disgust. Hume did not hesitate because he knew there had to be a negotiated settlement, that the IRA and its war could not be wished away, and he said so when it was not popular to think and talk in such terms. It is not an overstatement to say that he put his life and his party on the line for peace—something that is not fully recognised or remembered in all the euphoria and dizziness of the new political era of the DUP and Sinn Féin. As the Hume–Adams process stretched through the 1980s and into the 1990s, through the atrocities of Shankill and Greysteel, the UDA considered murdering Hume. That was the extent of the risk he took, yet he was vilified by many, including sections of the media, who watched from a safe distance and then pontificated about right and wrong. Hume is one of the principal makers of the new peace, one of those whose analysis helped others begin to think and talk their way out of the war. What if Hume had taken the easy option back then? What if he had turned his back and walked away? What would have been the consequences of that in our story of war and peace? That process of peace-building leading to the ceasefire of 1994 was obscured, buried beneath the bombs and the bullets. It was almost dismissed at the time in the worlds of politics and security because people could not see past the war and towards the peace. Hume said and did the right things at the right time, and had the patience and the vision for what was an exhausting journey. He was able to make the jigsaw in his mind and show others the pieces and the picture—even those who did not want to see.

Adams and McGuinness had been with the IRA from those earliest days of its war—young men in talks with the British in the 1970s, different men in the critical peace negotiations of 1997–2007 that eventually produced the Good Friday Agreement and, later, the historic deal with Paisley in the St Andrews Agreement. Not different in the sense of any selling out, as some might label it, but politically wiser and tuned into the realities of conflict resolution. Looking back with hindsight, what has their achievement been? It has been the delivery of the Republican movement into the peace process with the minimum of damage to its structure. Yes, they lost the dissidents at the start of that critical decade of negotiations, but those dissidents buried themselves in the slaughter of the Omagh bomb in August 1998. Inside republicanism, no credible alternative leadership—military or political—has emerged. The movement, by and large, has followed Adams and McGuinness out of war and towards peace. The IRA's contribution to this has been a series of peace initiatives—first ceasefires, then weapons inspections, then some decommissioning—that culminated in the formal ending of the armed campaign in July 2005 and, soon after, the putting beyond use of arms as a confirmation that the war was over. These, to quote an intelligence source, were the digestible chunks that had to be swallowed. Perhaps the one that stuck in the republican throat more than any other was the endorsement of policing in 2007. This, more than anything else, was making peace with the enemy. It was the very thing that proclaimed loudest that the war was over and the combatants were fully committed to peace.

Ian Paisley is a different man. He found a way out of his politics of 'never' and 'no' and into government with Martin McGuinness. His achievement is that, like Adams and McGuinness, he delivered the DUP into this new era with the minimum of damage to the party. At the moment he said yes, only a very few said no, the most significant being Jim Allister MEP. Peter Robinson, as successor to Paisley, now has to prove himself in political leadership.

I wonder what Tony Blair and Bertie Ahern were thinking as they watched it all? Could they really have expected this at the end of their ten-year project? This was the prize of all prizes, although that is not to minimise the significance of that first power-sharing Executive of David Trimble and Seamus Mallon. In the long peace process, that too was a significant moment in the post-Good Friday Agreement phase. But what we have now is a staggering move forward. Who would have dared imagine a working, workable DUP–Sinn Féin government? It has the look of Hume's vision of an 'agreed' Ireland. Harold Good, one of the Church witnesses to the IRA decommissioning of 2005, found the words to describe that moment in May 2007 when enemies entered a shared government and a shared future:

For me the most memorable image on the day was that of Ian Paisley and Martin McGuinness entering Parliament Buildings through that revolving door … Remember the hand of one gently navigating the other. The offering of respect and safe passage by one and acceptance by the other. In another context this would be considered a trivial incident, but for me this was the 'hand of history'—worth more than a thousand contrived handshakes.

This new arrangement was a long time in the making. It took almost five years to build after the collapse of the Ulster Unionist–sdlp-led Executive in the ira spy scandal that was Stormontgate. Trimble did not get out of Adams and McGuinness and the ira what Paisley got out of them. And for many, this remains a political mystery—that more was done for Paisley than for Trimble. Yet strangely, republicans feel more secure in this arrangement with the dup. Trimble was not in charge of all his party as the business of the Good Friday Agreement was rolled out—early prisoner releases, decommissioning not resolved, the question of police reforms to be addressed, a government with republicans. It was too much for many of Trimble's colleagues, and they refused to walk down that path with him. Indeed, some of those who refused to walk alongside Trimble later walked alongside Paisley in his party— another of the mysteries of political life after the Good Friday Agreement.

I think this new era of power-sharing is based on pragmatism. There was an electoral trend from 2003 that was pushing the dup and Sinn Féin towards each other and into government. Some saw the inevitability of that sooner than others. I was certain in 2004 that some of the most senior figures in the dup were working towards a political arrangement with Sinn Féin. I knew that because I was talking to them on a regular basis. There was a context, of course, including a convincing end to the armed campaign, decommissioning and a republican acceptance of policing. Adams and McGuinness, with the IRA leadership, delivered all three; Paisley said yes.

It is still too early to talk about trust. The question of the past must be explained by all sides, but for now, politically, something solid has been fashioned from the clay of negotiations that is nothing less than a masterpiece in conflict resolution. It has worked here in the context of the Irish peace process; parts of it could work elsewhere. Tony Blair, Bertie Ahern and Ian Paisley have all moved on from their positions of political leadership. Each in his own way made a significant contribution to the making of the peace. The model, the thinking, the experience, these are the things that can now be given to others. We have an unique opportunity now in Northern Ireland: to create from our shared burden of a bloody past the gift of a shared vision for future peace. That can be our legacy to the world. That war with no winners is over.

Appendix 1

Key extracts from Gerry Adams' speech, 6 April 2005

AN ADDRESS TO THE IRA

I want to speak directly to the men and women of Oglaigh na hEireann, the volunteer soldiers of the Irish Republican Army. In time of great peril you stepped into the Bearna Baoil, the gap of danger. When others stood idly by, you and your families gave your all, in defence of a risen people and in pursuit of Irish freedom and unity.

Against mighty odds you held the line and faced down a huge military foe, the British crown forces and their surrogates in the unionist death squads.

Eleven years ago the Army leadership ordered a complete cessation of military operations...

The Irish Republican Army has kept every commitment made by its leadership.

The most recent of these was last December when the IRA was prepared to support a comprehensive agreement. At that time the Army leadership said the implementation of this agreement would allow everyone, including the IRA, to take its political objectives forward by peaceful and democratic means.

That agreement perished on the rock of unionist intransigence...

For over thirty years the IRA showed that the British Government could not rule Ireland on its own terms.

You asserted the legitimacy of the right of the people of this island to freedom and independence.

Many of your comrades made the ultimate sacrifice.

Your determination, selflessness and courage have brought the freedom struggle towards its fulfilment.

That struggle can now be taken forward by other means. I say this with the authority of my office as President of Sinn Féin.

In the past I have defended the right of the IRA to engage in armed struggle. I did so because there was no alternative for those who would not bend the knee, or turn a blind eye to oppression, or for those who wanted a national republic.

Now there is an alternative.

I have clearly set out my view of what that alternative is. The way forward is by building political support for republican and democratic objectives across Ireland and by winning support for these goals internationally.

I want to use this occasion therefore to appeal to the leadership of Oglaigh na hEireann to fully embrace and accept this alternative.

Can you take courageous initiatives which will achieve your aims by purely political and democratic activity?

I know full well that such truly historic decisions can only be taken in the aftermath of intense internal consultation. I ask that you initiate this as quickly as possible.

Appendix 2

Key extracts from IRA Endgame Statement, 28 July 2005

The leadership of Oglaigh na hEireann has formally ordered an end to the armed campaign. This will take effect from 4.00pm this afternoon.

All IRA units have been ordered to dump arms.

All volunteers have been instructed to assist the development of purely political and democratic programmes through exclusively peaceful means. Volunteers must not engage in any other activities whatsoever.

The IRA leadership has also authorised our representative to engage with the IICD (Independent International Commission on Decommissioning) to complete the process to verifiably put its arms beyond use in a way which will further enhance public confidence and to conclude this as quickly as possible. We have invited two independent witnesses, from the Protestant and Catholic Churches to testify to this.

The Army Council took these decisions following an unprecedented internal discussion and consultation process with IRA units and volunteers...

The outcome of our consultations show very strong support among IRA volunteers for the Sinn Féin peace strategy...

We reiterate our view that the armed struggle was entirely legitimate...

The issue of the defence of nationalist and republican communities has been raised with us. There is a responsibility on society to ensure that there is no re-occurrence of the pogroms of 1969 and the early 1970s...

The IRA is fully committed to the goals of Irish unity and independence and to building the republic outlined in the 1916 Proclamation...

There is now an unprecedented opportunity to utilise the considerable energy and goodwill which there is for the peace process. This comprehensive series of unparalleled initiatives is our contribution to this and to the continued endeavours to bring about independence and unity for the people of Ireland.

P. O'Neill

Appendix 3
IRA Decommissioning Statement, 26 September 2005

The leadership of Oglaigh na hEireann announced on July 28th that we had authorised our representative to engage with the IICD (Independent International Commission on Decommissioning) to complete the process to verifiably put arms beyond use. The IRA leadership can now confirm that the process of putting our arms beyond use has been completed.

P. O'Neill

Appendix 4

Key extracts from motion to Sinn Féin Árd Fheis, 28 January 2007

The responsibility of the police is to defend and uphold the rights of citizens.

In order to fulfil this role they require critical support. Sinn Féin reiterates our support for An Garda Síochána and commits fully to:

- Support for the PSNI and the criminal justice system;
- Hold the police and criminal justice systems north and south fully to account, both democratically and legally, on the basis of fairness, impartiality and objectivity;
- Authorise our elected representatives to participate in local policing structures in the interests of justice, the quality of life for the community and to secure policing with the community as the core function of the PSNI, and actively encouraging everyone in the community to cooperate fully with the police services in tackling crime in all areas and actively supporting all the criminal justice institutions;
- The devolution of policing and justice to the Assembly;
- Equality and human rights at the heart of the new dispensation and to pursue a shared future in which the culture, rights and aspirations of all are respected and valued free from sectarianism, racism and intolerance.

(An IRA Army Convention preceded the Árd Fheis, on 26–27 January.)

Key extracts from Paisley–Adams Statements, 26 March 2007, at joint news conference announcing restoration of devolution on 8 May 2007

REV. IAN PAISLEY:

On Saturday the DUP Executive overwhelmingly endorsed a motion committing our party to support and participate fully in government in May this year. This is a binding resolution...

Today we have agreed with Sinn Féin that this date will be Tuesday 8 May 2007.

As the largest party in Northern Ireland we are committed to playing a full part in all the institutions and delivering the best future for all of the people of Northern Ireland.

In the period before devolution we will participate fully with the other parties to the Executive in making full preparations for the restoration of devolution on 8 May.

This meeting represents an important step on the road to the setting up of an Executive in six weeks' time.

It has been a constructive engagement and we have agreed that in the weeks between now and the restoration of devolution on 8 May there is important preparatory work to be carried out so that local ministers can hit the ground running.

This will include regular meetings between the future First and Deputy First Ministers (Ian Paisley and Martin McGuinness)…

After a long and difficult time in our province I believe that enormous opportunities lie ahead for our province…

I want to make it clear that I am committed to delivering not only for those who voted for the DUP but for all the people of Northern Ireland.

We must not allow our justified loathing of the horrors and tragedies of the past to become a barrier to creating a better and more stable future for our children.

In looking to that future we must never forget those who have suffered during the dark period from which we are, please God, now emerging.

We owe it to them to craft and build the best future possible and ensure there is genuine support for all those who are still suffering.

GERRY ADAMS:

I want to begin my remarks by welcoming the statement by Ian Paisley.

While it is disappointing that the institutions of the Good Friday Agreement have not been restored today, I believe the agreement reached between Sinn Féin and the DUP, including the unequivocal commitment made by their party executive and reiterated today to the restoration of political institutions on 8 May, marks the beginning of a new era of politics on this island…

The relationships between the people of this island have been marred by centuries of discord, conflict, hurt and tragedy.

In particular this has been the sad history of orange and green.

Sinn Féin is about building a new relationship between orange and green and all the other colours, where every citizen can share and have equality of ownership of a peaceful, prosperous and just future.

There are still many challenges, many difficulties to be faced. But let us be clear. The basis of the agreement between Sinn Féin and the DUP follows Ian Paisley's unequivocal and welcome commitment to support and participate fully in the political institutions on 8 May…

We are very conscious of the many people who have suffered.

We owe it to them to build the best future possible.

It is a time for generosity, a time to be mindful of the common good and of the future of all our people.

I am pleased to say that collectively we have created the potential to build a new, harmonious and equitable relationship between nationalists and republicans and unionists as well as the rest of the people of the island of Ireland.

Sinn Féin will take nothing for granted in the days and weeks ahead, but we will do all that we can to ensure a successful outcome and we ask everyone to support us in our efforts.

Appendix 6

Key extracts from UVF Endgame Statement, 3 May 2007

Following a direct engagement with all units and departments of our organisation, the leadership of the Ulster Volunteer Force and Red Hand Commando today make public the outcome of our three year consultation process.

We do so against a backdrop of increasing community acceptance that the mainstream republican offensive has ended; that the six principles upon which our ceasefire was predicated are maintained; that the principle of consent has been firmly established and thus, that the Union remains safe...

As of twelve midnight, Thursday 3 May 2007, the Ulster Volunteer Force and Red Hand Commando will assume a non-military, civilianised, role.

To consolidate this fundamental change in outlook we have addressed the methodology of transformation from a military to a civilian organisation by implementing the following measures in every operational and command area:

All recruitment has ceased.

Military training has ceased.

Targeting has ceased and all intelligence rendered obsolete.

All Active Service Units have been deactivated.

All ordnance (weapons) has been put beyond reach and the Independent International Commission on Decommissioning (IICD) instructed accordingly...

We reaffirm our opposition to all criminality and instruct our volunteers to cooperate fully with the lawful authorities in all possible instances. Moreover, we state unequivocally, that any volunteer engaged in criminality does so in direct contravention of Brigade Command...

We have taken the above measures in an earnest attempt to augment the return of accountable democracy to the people of Northern Ireland and as such, to engender confidence that the constitutional question has now been firmly settled.

In doing so we reaffirm the legitimacy of our tactical response to violent nationalism yet reiterate the sincere expression of abject and true remorse to all innocent victims of the conflict.

Captain William Johnston, Adjutant

Appendix 7
Key extracts from UDA Endgame Statement, 11 November 2007

The Ulster Defence Association believes that the war is over and we are now in a new democratic dispensation that will lead to permanent political stability, but we believe the political parties and the political institutions are themselves still in a period of transition…

The ballot box and the political institutions must be the greatest weapons…

All active service units of the Ulster Freedom Fighters will as from 12pm tonight stand down with all military intelligence destroyed, and as a consequence of this all weaponry will be put beyond use (**this did not mean decommissioned**) …

The battle flags of the Ulster Freedom Fighters will be furled in a hope that they may never have to see light of day again, but stand in readiness…

It is the duty of every member to understand that to be involved in crime or criminality is to undermine the cause. We have had those who joined our ranks for political reasons; these men went on to give great sacrifice and brought honour to the organisation and gained the respect of their comrades. But there have been those who joined our ranks for crime and self gain. These people must be rooted out…

Index